FATHERHOOD

WILLIAM McINNES

FATHERHOOD

STORIES ABOUT BEING A DAD

hachette
AUSTRALIA

These are my memories. The names and descriptions of some people have been changed so that they too can preserve their own memories, in their own ways.

William McInnes

hachette
AUSTRALIA

Published in Australia and New Zealand in 2018
by Hachette Australia
(an imprint of Hachette Australia Pty Limited)
Level 17, 207 Kent Street, Sydney NSW 2000
www.hachette.com.au

10 9 8 7 6 5 4 3 2 1

A catalogue record for this book is available from the National Library of Australia

ISBN: 978 0 7336 3554 0

Cover design by Christabella Designs
Cover photograph by James Calderaro
Inside cover photograph by Sarah Watt
Internal photos courtesy William McInnes and Shutterstock
Text design by Bookhouse, Sydney
Typeset in 12.35/18.4 pt Bembo Std by Bookhouse, Sydney
Printed and bound in Australia by McPherson's Printing Group

To fathers and their children everywhere

and

Amanda

CONTENTS

Author's Note   ix

1   Father's Day Presents   1
    A Letter to My Daughter   35
2   By Humpybong Creek   42
3   Other People's Fathers, Part 1   79
4   Other People's Fathers, Part 2   113
5   The Things You Think About When Shopping   154
6   Father Karma   192
    A Letter to My Son   223
7   Father Knows Best   229
8   My Rifle, My Pony and Me   268

Acknowledgements   293

AUTHOR'S NOTE

This book isn't a manual of how to be a better father, or how to be a father at all. It's just stories about the strange state that men can find themselves in, with all its adventures and permutations, its ups and downs, of how remembered events echo down through the years, of how suddenly a penny drops and you understand something a little more about that state of Fatherhood.

1

FATHER'S DAY PRESENTS

There are only two presents I can remember giving my father for Father's Day. One was a painting on a large piece of butcher's paper that I did at primary school. It was entitled a 'Portrait of Father' and my classmates and I had all painted one during the week of Father's Day.

The local Woolies was running a competition and was going to put some of the portraits in its front windows. Amazingly, somebody chose my 'Portrait of Father'. A head smoking a pipe.

I can vaguely remember my father having the odd durry on Boxing Day and at parties, and I recall he shared a smoke with a car salesman after he bought what turned out to be a deeply unreliable and shiftless Holden ute.

Like most motors in used car lots, it had had a sign written in a professional hand describing the auto in a few words. Usually these were generic signs with things like 'V8 Power', 'Automatic', 'This Week's Special' or 'Classy' and were swapped around the various cars until they were bought.

The Holden ute, with a strange plywood cover over the tray that looked like it had come off a covered wagon from some black-and-white TV western, had never been adorned with any of these signs. Instead it had been heralded in purple lettering as 'A Canny Buy!'.

My father had muttered about this ute for a few weeks, sometimes around the barbecue or in the kitchen or at the table.

While other cars might have been newer and flashier, he was taken with the idea that this was the thinking punter's pick – a canny buy; the choice for the buyer who knew what was what.

My mother laughed. 'It's just another sign, just something they stick in a window, you silly man.'

'No, love, it's not. I know what I'm about,' my father said.

'You are talking about the one with the purple sign in the window?' my mother had asked.

'My word. A canny buy,' said my father.

'Cardinals only wear purple at Lent . . . Or when they're mourning.'

My father waved his hand. 'Christ alive, we're talking about a ute, not our boy Norm.'

'I'm just saying,' said my mother.

'We'll be right.'

Our boy Norm was the name my father gave to Cardinal Norman Gilroy, the Labor-leaning Catholic priest who had become Australia's first cardinal.

Notwithstanding my mother's misgivings about the cardinal's purple hue, the old man did indeed buy the Canny Buy, but as he puffed on that fag offered by the salesman I think he was starting to have doubts.

The salesman seemed a tad too eager and relieved, almost offering the cigarette as a way of calming himself down as much as celebrating the deal, as if he couldn't believe he had found a buyer for the Canny Buy.

In time, the ute's true character was revealed and my mother never let my father forget the purple sign. 'I told you!' she would say when the car wouldn't start or hissed like an asthmatic.

My father referred to the ute as 'Norman's Lament' when he was feeling fatalistic but more often than not he simply swore and muttered under his breath, 'Canny buy, my arse.'

•

Apart from that dart to celebrate the purchase of Norman's Lament, the only other evidence of the old man chuffing came in the form of a photograph from his service days, with a cigarette in one hand as he stood in front of a row of tents. That's as far as his smoking went. So I have no idea why I painted my father smoking a pipe, although there was a loose interpretation of 'fathers' in quite a few of the works.

One kid got into trouble for making his father a pirate, complete with an eye patch and parrot on his shoulder, when we all knew that his dad worked as a bitumen layer with the council. Another boy, whose dad ran a newsagent down at Woody Point, painted his father as a vampire with fangs and a cape. So, in the scheme of things, a pipe was a pretty mild stretch and was inspired, I'm sure, by the fact that somewhere on some TV show or movie, some incarnation of a father had smoked a pipe — so that was good enough for me, and for Woolies too.

It seemed slightly ironic that an imagined portrait of my father should adorn a window in Woolies, for I doubt my father ever set foot inside Woolworths, or any other supermarket for that matter. Shopping wasn't his domain, it was the world of my mother.

Later perhaps, when the renovated Woolies stood on the site of the old shop at Margate, he would have followed my mother around on a shopping trip, tottering along with unsteady steps, his body failing as well as his mind, dementia descending around him like a cloak.

But all that was in the future. Back then, my make-believe pipe-smoking portrait of my father hung in Woolworths and I was given a hanky as a prize. I kept the hanky and gave the butcher's paper portrait to my father.

He nodded and said, 'Who's this then?'

'It's you.'

He nodded again and said, 'Right then.' And patted me on the head.

•

The other present I can recall giving my father was from some dreadful manual arts class in the early years of high school. A cheese board.

It was the only thing I constructed in manual arts that didn't crumble to pieces within minutes of my completing it.

To say my efforts at manual arts were challenged was an understatement. 'Not quite right' was the style of which I was a master. I had produced a series of creations that ranked highly in the pantheon of dire and my lack of ability in measuring, cutting, joining and riveting played heavily upon me, because it was as if I was failing in being a functioning human being. In particular, a man, for manual arts was what men did.

In the early days of my secondary education, when prepubescence was giving way to puberty and the changes that were beginning to take place in our bodies were bubbling away like some fermenting hillbilly's brew, where body and mind were heading six different directions at once, there was a sense of treading unsteady ground.

I had an inkling that manual arts and navigating hormonal development might be a bit of a minefield from an incident in the final year of primary school. It was a Friday afternoon and a group of us boys sat weaving baskets for an hour. On these Friday afternoons students who couldn't swim were sent off to the local pool for lessons while those of us who could swim were stuck by some bike racks dipping bits of wicker cane into tubs of water and then weaving them into some form of basket.

It had the feel of a scene from a war movie where shell-shocked Tommies from the trenches of Verdun sat silently weaving in rehabilitation classes.

On that particular Friday afternoon, two boys who would normally have gone swimming joined us shell-shocked weavers because they were unfit for swimming duty. Barry Sphinx, a great hulking boy who had been kept down a year and whose nickname was Balloon Dacks because of the inflated nature of his stubbie shorts, was there because he had an ear infection. The other boy, Darren Lawrence, had the beginnings of a cold, or 'the sniffles' as he himself put it. Barry Sphinx seemed quite happy dunking the cane in the tubs for us weavers, but Darren Lawrence simply sat staring at Barry.

He turned and whispered to me, 'That boy Barry . . . Barry Sphinx.' He paused as if incredulous about what he was about to say. 'He has hairs, lots of hairs around his . . . around his big dickie bird.'

I stopped my weaving and looked at Darren and then at the Sphinx.

Well, if he was going to call a cold 'the sniffles', of course he'd call a prick a 'dickie bird'. I didn't know what to think about his use of the descriptive word 'big'. Instead, I looked at Barry Sphinx.

A teacher patted him on the shoulder.

'You look like you know what you're about, Barry. You could teach a few of these others how to handle cane. Boys, take note.'

I knew the teacher meant boys like me, for he had stopped beside me earlier and looked down at my effort. I knew my basket wasn't much chop, but this teacher decided to point it out to me just in case I didn't understand.

'What a sad, soggy lopsided thing. That basket is devoid of spirit.' Then he added a phrase that would haunt me throughout my manual arts training. 'Your father's a builder, isn't he?'

The words hung in the air, summing up the hopelessness of my position.

A part of me thought this teacher wasn't one to speak, for he hadn't actually taught us how to weave the baskets; he was just there to keep us quiet. Another teacher had given us a demonstration using a series of baskets in different forms of gestation. He was the basket man, but once his formative weaving wisdom was given he disappeared back into his classroom.

This present teacher was a fellow who walked with a limp and drove a car so tiny that it seemed almost to be a novelty toy pulled from the bowels of a breakfast cereal pack. Norman's Lament seemed like a Roller compared to the teacher's funny little Hillman Minx. I had also seen him shopping in Woolies after school one Friday as I walked alongside Mum, and this was a sure sign to my tiny brain that he wasn't a proper grown-up man.

He had nodded to my mother as he walked past for he had taught one of my sisters, and my mother nodded in return. I'd also seen my mum occasionally give him some leftover salad rolls from the school tuckshop when she was on duty there. I had never asked why she and the other mothers did this, I just thought he was scamming a free eat. He had yelled at a couple of boys once when they suggested that he should pay for the leftovers.

'He's got a shopping list,' said my mother that Friday in the supermarket, as if this was some profound event.

'Dad doesn't go shopping,' I said.

'Unless it's for useless bleeding cars like Norman's Lament, so that's a good thing, I suppose. God knows what he'd come home with,' she muttered as she looked at the tins of State jam.

Not taking into account the Canny Buy, my father, it must be said, had form here. One Christmas when my mother was laid up with a severe bout of morning sickness carrying her fifth child, which turned out to be me, my father was deputised to go off and buy some presents for his four children.

He had come back very happy with himself because he'd managed to purchase five bags of cement and two of lime, which were on special at the BBC Hardware store. It was an offer too good to walk away from. He'd completely forgotten the presents and my mother had had to race, retching, to the shops at the very last minute to fill the stockings.

But that was okay. My dad was a grown-up man – he wasn't supposed to shop in supermarkets.

As I watched the teacher with the limp in the supermarket, I felt a little tap behind my head. It was my mother flicking her palm against my melon.

'That man's a widower.' I looked at her blankly and she continued. 'His wife died, so he has to do the shopping for his family, all right? He's got a couple of little girls to look after as well as teaching the likes of you, so just watch yourself.'

And she went back to the tins of State jam.

I didn't say anything.

But when the teacher stood before me praising Barry's cane-drowning skills I remembered him paddling down the aisle with his funny limping walk wrangling his trolley.

It seemed to me only someone as odd as Barry Sphinx could understand the complexity of basket creation, that he could be as one with wicker cane.

'Like a beard,' whispered Darren Lawrence, interrupting my thoughts. 'Hairs like Captain Haddock's beard.'

Whatever one could say about Darren, he certainly had a graphic way of putting things. The idea that Barry Sphinx had hairs in his balloon dacks like Tintin's blustering nautical friend and offsider Captain Haddock was startling. I couldn't help but think, 'Blue blistering barnacles' as the good captain himself might have said.

Back at home, the image lingered. In a quiet moment, I found my father in the backyard and I spoke about Barry Sphinx as the old man stood burning bits and pieces of stuff in the incinerator.

'Hairs, hey?' he said.

'Lots, apparently.'

My father poked at the flames.

'Like a beard,' I said.

He raised his eyebrows.

'He's got Captain Haddock in his pants.'

My father turned to me and stared, his brow furrowed. 'What?'

I stared back, not quite sure what to make of his tone.

My father tried to join the dots. 'Haddock? As in fish?'

I had no idea on what grown-up tangent he was travelling, so I told him who Captain Haddock and Tintin were.

My father rolled his tongue around his mouth a little. 'Captain Haddock from the comics. And your mate Barry Sphinx has got a bit of Captain Haddock going on downstairs.'

Barry wasn't my mate, but this conversation was proving a little trickier than I had thought it might be, so I decided not to say anything and instead tried to give my best searching-for-knowledge look.

'You get a gander of this yourself?' My father paused. I thought a smile touched the corner of his mouth. 'Of his . . . uh . . . of this Haddock paddock?'

I shook my head and told him it was Darren Lawrence who had seen the hairs when they were getting changed for swimming.

'Darren Lawrence, eh?'

My father stopped poking the fire and looked at me.

I looked back.

Then I thought I should fill him in.

'They go swimming, usually on a Friday, but Barry Sphinx had an earache and Darren had the sniffles.'

My father nodded.

'Darren had the sniffles, eh? And he's got the gossip on Barry and his pants beard.'

I stared.

'Well, it can happen. Yes. The mystery of the Sphinx,' he said very wisely. Then he sniffed a little and cleared his throat. 'Don't worry, son, you'll understand one day and your Captain Haddock's not too far off, I'd say.' And he nodded his head again.

He poked the fire a bit more and said into the flames very thoughtfully, 'Captain Haddock.' Then, as an afterthought, he tilted his head towards me slightly and said, 'Watch out for that Darren fella, will ya?'

I stared at him, not quite sure what he meant. He was about to say something else but thought better of it. After a while he spoke again.

'You want to burn something?'

I did. And I forgot about the mystery of the Sphinx as a bunch of old cardboard and yellowing *Courier Mail* newspapers crackled in the flames.

•

I felt a similar uneasiness about the manual arts class as I did about the Sphinx's Captain Haddock because the manual arts department exuded the certainty and confidence that was so alien to me. These were men who knew exactly how to take a piece of metal or timber and fashion it into an item that served a purpose. They worked miracles with bits of plywood and dowel to create a letter-holder or they'd take a piece of beaten tin and shape it into a perfect cylindrical scone-cutter, complete with a tiny arched handle riveted into the thickened fold on top. A 'utensil', the teachers called it.

In class, a teacher held up a thin tubular piece of plastic, then a hole punch, then a sheet of metal, then a hammer. 'These,' he bellowed, waving to the materials and tools like the models waved to the prizes on the quiz show *Sale of the Century*, 'will become THIS!'

He held up something that looked impressively neat and shiny. The class stared dumbfounded at this sorcery, even though some of us didn't know exactly what this impressive utensil actually was.

'A pot strainer, men! A pot strainer. Something to keep Mum happy.'

Apart from these pioneering manly skills, almost all the manual arts teachers were loud bears of men with incredibly neat writing and an aura of being impeccably tidy.

Even the one teacher who wasn't as loud and large as the others still exuded enough of these elemental manly qualities to appear to belong to this rare breed. Mr Smythe, one of the metalwork teachers, was a slight man no taller than us boys and very quietly spoken. He never wore shorts, but instead wore dark trousers and a white shirt, occasionally with a dark tie. His hair was slicked back with Brylcreem and his voice was a soothing monotone. He quietly roamed the benches of the workroom almost in the manner of Alec Guinness's Obi-Wan Kenobi, indicating with a point of one of his fingers how a scone-cutter could be brought to fruition.

While he passed on his wisdom with a wave of one hand, the fingers of his other would delicately roll a cigarette, smoothing down the tobacco, almost weaving the fibres and gently cupping the Tally-Ho paper as a perfect roll-your-own would appear, like a small lightsaber, to be caressed by his tongue and popped behind his right ear for later use.

These manual arts teachers seemed to belong on a higher plain of evolutionary development, and we boys looked upon them with a sense of fear and awe. Soon it would become apparent that some boys were worthy of the highest form of manual arts praise; they were deemed to be 'handy and adept'.

The rest of us unfinished beings, a collection of lanky, podgy, unwieldy and mostly supremely uncoordinated teenage boys, would do our best to navigate the treacherous obstacle course of woodwork, metalwork and the dark arts of technical drawing.

Technical drawing was a subject which confounded many. We sat in rooms with slanting desks and attempted to render elevations and scale dimensions of tables and chairs. Even worse were the floor plans and roof angles of imaginary houses we were asked to copy.

The subject was taught by a man who looked like a recruitment poster for manual arts teachers. He was stout with his business shorts slung around his gut and he always wore vertically striped shirts which would wrap around his stomach to give the impression of a spinnaker from a large yacht billowing with the sea wind on the homeward stretch to the line.

He was covered in a forest of hair except for his clean-shaven face, which grew darker by the hour with the encroaching day's growth from his body's scrubland. His nickname was Donger.

'That looks like a humpy, not a home, and your writing's like chook scratchings. You're not somebody from the back of beyond, McInnes.' And he shook his head and said the words I knew were coming. 'Your father's a builder, isn't he?'

I blushed and stared down at my slanting desk. The teacher moved on.

Some students, though, were deemed worthy of the highest praise the teachers could offer. The class would be called to attention after one of the manual arts masters had prowled around the room and stopped by a workbench. 'Men!' would be the call and we boys would gather and stare as another boy's scone-cutter would be held aloft by the teacher in front of us as some fine trophy, 'This utensil is well made. This is what you are after.'

•

Looking back on it, I can see that giving boys the chance to create something out of bits and pieces of plywood and tin could give them a sense of achievement.

But it was also an exercise in insanity – the 'utensils' were uniformly crap, and even the ones that were correctly made by the teachers were, on closer inspection, completely ill-suited for the purposes for which they were intended, no matter how 'handy and adept' the maker might be.

A flat pot strainer with a thin piece of plastic covering its handle did nothing more than scald the holder while the overflow of hot water from the pot would give the person something to go on with. The letter-holders disintegrated, the scone-cutter rusted and left odd specks of metal detritus on dough if it was ever used in anger. The people who were adept at making utensils probably would have approved of the strange plywood wagon cover adorning the back tray of Norman's Lament, for it was as useless.

All this, though, was with the benefit of hindsight. At the time, the trauma of having to try and emulate these manual arts masters to their constant refrain of 'Your father's a builder, isn't he?' seemed torturous.

And along the way there were unintended consequences, such as the dreaded scone-cutter incident.

In metalwork, the normally quiet Jedi Smythe was facing a Herculean task to ensure that at least one boy in my class completed a scone-cutter. As the term had progressed, Mr Smythe had seemed to become more drawn and tired, the scone-cutter campaign weighing on him heavily.

We were the worst class at the school by far and would cannibalise each other's efforts – and pinch a part of someone else's cutter if it seemed to fit better than our own. This had been going on for most of that first term's foray into the dark arts of scone-cutter creation. Jedi Smythe decided to make each of us identify the pieces of our scone-cutter with a small stamp. This was, I thought, slightly extreme.

'Now, boys,' said Jedi Smythe, in his pleasant tones as he made a roll-your-own in his left hand. 'Choose a stamp to mark your work, there's no point in taking each other's bits and pieces, it proves nothing.'

There was a tumbler filled with different punch stamps from which we were supposed to choose an individual mark, but teenage boys being teenage boys, not one of us thought to take a different stamp, for that would have taken too much initiative and presence of mind. Instead each boy used the same brand, a little star, to identify our pieces of scone-cutter. When one student had finished making his mark, the same stamp was passed to the next student.

Why it was never noticed can probably only be explained by the assumption that any given group of human beings could not be as stupid as that class. Such a lack of suspicion had consequences though, for Jedi Smythe, usually the calmest of the teachers, became increasingly irate over the weeks as he worked his way through the bits and pieces of tin left on the shelves as we all hovered around scavenging.

'You, the tall boy, McInnes, the builder's boy,' he said evenly.

I turned with a few bits of illicit scone merchandise.

'Let me see them.' I proffered my stolen tin bits and he saw they were all stamped with a star.

'These aren't yours, boy.' He rolled another cigarette, and I noticed that his durries were becoming a little more ragged and less defined. He scrunched up his smoke.

I nodded that they were mine.

'They're all correctly measured, boy, they can't be yours.'

I nodded that they were.

He rolled another fag, even more unruly than the first. 'Let me see your mark.'

I showed him my star stamp. He fossicked through the pieces of tin and he made a noise in his throat.

He stared at me and the stamp.

Mr Smythe rolled an invisible durry, nodded and walked around the room very slowly. He was extremely quiet for the rest of the lesson. At the end, when we walked out, he put the smoke in his mouth and stared at me. He was about to say something but as he took the rollie from his mouth, half the makings stayed on his lip and then disappeared down his throat.

He staggered over to where we had placed our scone-cutters and picked a few up and looked at the stamps as we filed out the door for little lunch.

It was Howard Barber who found him by the incinera-
tors, a place preferred by students who wanted to have a
quick chuff on the sly with tailor-made cigarettes, usually
Winfield or Escort, which earned them the name of the
Incinerator Club.

Teachers would occasionally go to the Incinerator Club
to nab an errant student or maybe even to have a smoke
themselves.

Apparently, Jedi Smythe had been about to have a
man-to-man chat with a few members of the Incinerator
Club and had taken a deep suck on his smoke and promptly
exploded into a coughing fit while shaking as evidence in
the open palm of his hand a few pieces of scone-cutter.

'McInnes's scone-cutter —' He had stopped and then
belched a river of smoke and collapsed, his hand balling
into a tight fist around the scone-cutter metal.

He'd suffered a heart attack, and even though Howard
knew the dangers of being caught openly with a lit cigarette,
he bravely ran off to the staffroom and raised the alarm.
Apparently he explained away the lit Winnie Blue he had
in his fingers by saying he had picked up a lit smoke as he
walked past the incinerator and thought he should put it
in a bin. As the teachers ran to help Jedi Smythe, Howard
stayed in the staffroom and finished the fag, ashing it in a

cup on the staffroom desk and earning himself a certain status amongst the rest of us.

The fallen Jedi was taken to hospital and never returned to school. Howard Barber was praised at school assembly and another teacher came and oversaw the completion of our communal scone-cutters.

I don't know if I was the only boy in that metalwork class who felt a bit guilty about Mr Smythe but the news went around amongst students – and parents – that it was our scone-cutters that nearly did him in.

My father fronted me in the backyard.

'Hey you,' he nodded his head at me, 'be careful what you bring home from school – we don't want any lethal weapons coming here.'

I stared a bit gormlessly.

'No killer scone-cutters. You got that?' And he winked.

Was he joking? I wasn't sure.

'It wasn't just my scone-cutter –'

The old man rolled his tongue around his mouth, then nodded his head. 'Don't worry, sunshine, poor old Stan Smythe smokes like there's no tomorrow, something was bound to go bung sooner or later.'

My father needn't have worried, I didn't bring the scone-cutter home and, even though I finished it by picking amongst the sadder bits of metal, I didn't want it in the house any more than he did; it was cursed. I'm sure I wasn't the only boy who tossed their 'utensil' into the bin.

It was woodwork where I completed the one item that I felt I should bring home and, unlike the killer scone-cutters, it was all my own work.

My mother thought it would make a nice Father's Day present for my old man. 'He'd like to see what you've made. Anyway, it's the thought that counts.'

It was a lamentable effort. The handle wasn't straight and instead of the hexagonal design required, it was a misshapen particle-board disaster, the Richard the Third of cheese boards:

Deformed, unfinish'd, sent before my time
Into this breathing world, scarce half made up,
And that so lamely and unfashionable
That dogs bark at me as I halt by them.

Well, if a dog was going to bark at any cheese board it would be mine. And as the day came closer to take the cheese board home after they were graded, the manual arts teacher's words rang in my ears.

The fact that my father was a builder only exacerbated the awfulness of my cheese board. All the implied criticism of the teacher's words was obvious. Not only wasn't my work good enough, I wasn't good enough and my father would see this in the evidence I was to present to him in the form of my Richard the Third cheese board.

There was a truly terrifying manual arts teacher – a tall, fair-skinned man, with lank ginger hair sheared into a rather childlike bowl cut and with great veins that seemed set to explode from his muscular legs. He held my cheese board in his hands and beckoned me with a nod of his head to come and collect my piece of woodwork.

He was terrifying because he seemed to be some sort of hybrid between student and teacher. He was the youngest of all the manual arts teachers, and even though he followed their standard dress – rubber-soled shoes, long socks with a pen or metal pencil tucked in the top, business shorts, a short-sleeved shirt and a tie – there was something about his manner that made him seem closer in age to us students than the other teachers. He yelled as much as the other teachers and was full of threats of thick ears and of us boys not 'coming the raw prawn' with him, yet at the same time there were caveats – his voice, though loud, had a nasal quality, as if he'd just inhaled a helium balloon or as though his voice had only just broken.

And when he threatened us with a thick ear it felt more like a Chinese burn was on its way, where hands were placed on your forearm and then twisted in different directions. No adult would threaten with a Chinese burn, but a schoolyard tough might, like one of the older boys who had kept up with manual arts into the senior years because they were 'technically minded' or, in the words of my friend Beetle O'Brien, 'as thick as pig shit'.

And even though it was said that this teacher was a woodchop competitor, with a strong physique, apart from his ginger haircut he seemed to be otherwise hairless. All adult men seemed to balloon with body hair, as exemplified by Donger, but with his odd haircut the hybrid teacher seemed, the Barry Sphinxes of the world aside, not unlike the students he taught.

'You going to give this cheese board to your old man? The builder?'

I nodded.

He smirked.

'Good luck with that then.' And he sniggered a little. 'He'll be very proud.'

It was obvious, even to me, that my cheese board wasn't much chop and I couldn't see the point of this hybrid teacher taking the time to rub it in.

He looked like he was about to say more but thought better of it and just stared at me.

A shadow of doubt fell across my tiny brain; maybe my father would be as dismissive of my efforts as this teacher, he'd laugh at me and crush the uncertainly glued plywood before my eyes with his great paws.

Nevertheless, I presented it to him.

'What's this, then?' my old man asked.

'A letter-holder?' I said hesitatingly. Even I wasn't sure what the thing I had made was supposed to be.

'Right then,' he said and gave me a pat on the arm. 'Beauty.' He held it in his hands like some tiny tennis racquet. 'This . . . cheese board,' he said slowly, 'this is something.' He nodded like he often did, for no particular reason.

I didn't know if he was impressed. I suspected not, but the fact that he made no derogatory comment about its merits as a piece of construction made me think I had managed to get away with something.

I even felt slightly better about myself, as if in some way my father approved of my effort by merely ignoring it.

•

The next manual arts class after Father's Day the hybrid teacher asked me if I'd given 'that thing', meaning the cheese board, to my father.

I told him I had.

'How'd you go?'

I shrugged my shoulders and said, 'Yeah, okay, sir. He liked it.'

The hybrid teacher looked at me and after a while said softly, 'Good on him.'

Then he went to the front of the class and shouted at us for the next forty-five minutes as we endeavoured to make an ornamental placemat.

Not long after, in the school holidays, I walked around the local agricultural show trying to come to terms with a dagwood dog I had just bought. Dagwood dogs were always slightly unwieldy at best and I had made a bit of a blue when wandering around the schools exhibit with my huge battered shillelagh bleeding with a fountain of tomato sauce. Two dollops had fallen on the floor and splattered close to the town's manual arts display, collected from the various schools on the peninsula. Before I was moved on by a steward, I saw that my classmate Kevin McNamara had won a first place for his scone-cutter. It shone with a burnished sheen and a little paper certificate and, even though I felt a twinge of guilt about Jedi Smythe, I couldn't help but think that a part of my work, indeed the whole class's work, had been recognised by the judges.

I decided it was easier to eat the battered hot dog on a stick dripping with tomato sauce in a stationary sitting position instead of staggering around trying to shove it in my gob. I settled at the woodchops where the seats were only half full for the heats, the finals being what brought the crowds. I saw one of my friends' brothers who was at uni. He was with his girlfriend and they both had long wavy hair and were studiously unkempt and a bit 'cool'. They were laughing at the competitors. Mostly these men had short back and sides and looked a little odd with their singlets, Dunlop Volleys and gleaming axes.

'It's so silly,' said my friend's elder brother. 'Sort of Freudian, hey?'

His girlfriend giggled. 'Oh, come on.'

'No, look, these guys in their ornamental uniforms standing before a phallic symbol and preparing to hack away at it, emasculating themselves!' He cuddled his girlfriend.

'Or their patriarchal complex! Cutting their fathers down to size!' She laughed again.

I didn't quite know what was going on, but I knew enough to know they were having a go, which was a bit odd to me as I quite liked the woodchops.

It was a standing block competition and hardly any handicap was called, the highest being a count of five so even I knew that this must be a very junior round.

My friend's brother laughed and said, 'Which one?'

His girlfriend pointed at a competitor at the end of the line. 'That one with the little boy's haircut.'

I was surprised to see the hybrid teacher. He was much older than his competitors, but not much better.

We had thought him a champion axeman, but he was coming last. His axe blows stuck in the wood, making a squeaking noise as he jerkily tried to wrench the blade from the block. He was trying to go too fast, his arms bulging but his angles were too shallow, he had no purchase on the wood.

He did look a bit silly, I supposed. His blows became slower after the winner had finished and soon his strikes took on a plaintive sound as the axe became stuck after each effort.

'Give it a rest, son, you had a crack,' said a man leaning over the fence. He was dressed in the same outfit as the hybrid teacher only he wore a jacket with a state representative logo upon it. He looked very much like my manual arts teacher, but older. I guessed he was the teacher's father and the real champion axeman.

The hybrid teacher stopped, looked at his father and slowly took the axe out of the block. A marshal came and finished the block off with a chainsaw to make ready for the next round.

The cuddling couple giggled again and started kissing.

The hybrid teacher looked down at his axe and up at his father, but somebody had called his dad away, so he simply stood there, looking a little lonely.

Why, I wondered, did he bother if he wasn't much chop? It was the holidays. He looked pretty miserable. Then he laughed a little to himself: it looked like the time he'd asked me if I was taking the cheese board home to my father, and whether I thought my old man would be pleased with it. At the time I thought it had been a bit of a snigger, now it just looked sort of rueful and sad. Maybe he just wanted to make his father happy. I took a bite of my dagwood dog.

I remembered his face when he'd asked me how my old man had taken his Father's Day present. How he'd said 'Good on him' softly when I said my dad had liked it.

Perhaps he was going to say that it had been enough that I'd had a go and that it didn't matter that I wasn't as good as my father, it was just a funny little cheese board. For the hybrid teacher knew what it was like not to be as good as his father at something.

Maybe that was what he would have said.

•

I'm sure I gave my old man other presents but for some reason these were the two I remember. Perhaps it was because they were so dreadful – the cheese board should almost have been enough to have had me committed. But, more to the point, I think I remember them because of the manner with which they were accepted. A mixture of good humour and him not caring a flying fig, as if he had other things to be doing.

Or as if he thought that Father's Day was a bit of a joke, had a bit of an added-on feel to it, a poorer cousin of Mother's Day. Even today, people spend more on Mother's Day gifts than they do on Father's Day presents and that seems to be okay with all concerned. Fathers generally chin it and get on with their Sunday.

The days of Dad being given a new spanner set so he can happily change the oil or spark plugs or whatever it was that fathers would do under a car bonnet, are long gone, a retailers' retro wish list. Hardly anyone does anything to their cars these days except sit in them.

The only time I ever saw my father use a tool of any kind on a motor vehicle was when he would grab a hammer and belt the starter on the engine of Norman's Lament. He would give it a few healthy taps and then climb into the cabin, turn the ignition and wait for the car to sputter into life. Then he would whistle, laughing as if he'd won the lottery, and say, 'Better than a cup of coffee to get you going. Bastard of a thing and I'll be buggered how it works, but chucks away!' And off he would drive.

Perhaps Father's Day is just a bit of fun, a retailers' date more than anything, but as I get older a part of me hopes that on those Father's Days my father knew I loved him, regardless of pipe portraits and deformed cheese boards.

For it strikes me now that it is nice to be able to tell your old man you love him and maybe even nicer for him to hear it, for each time my own children have said those words to me it makes me feel that way, and I wonder if he felt that too.

About six months after my father died, my mother told me there was a box of bits and pieces to collect. She had collected items that were my father's and divvied them between her five children. 'There were some things I thought you all might like.'

In my box I found, amongst other things, a pair of cufflinks, some of his how-to-vote cards from when he stood for the local council, some of his thick square carpentry pencils, an old tie, and a programme from a 1973 rugby test between Australia and Tonga which was the first 'big game' of footy I had ever seen. It was also the first and only time I heard my father drop the 'F bomb'.

We had driven into Brisbane to Ballymore to watch the test in the wet. Amazingly Tonga had won 16–11. My father said nothing on most of the trip home as he sat behind the wheel trying to comprehend what had happened. It was only after we had passed Sandgate and were driving across Hayes Inlet along the long and bumpy Hornibrook Highway when he gave voice to his thoughts, muttering in astonishment, 'Tonga . . . (*hump*) . . . Fucking . . . (*hump*) . . . Tonga . . . (*hump*) . . . Fuck.'

There were a few other bits and pieces in the box and then, at the bottom, an old friend. A utensil. My Richard the Third cheese board. My father had kept it, it hadn't disintegrated. In fact, he had used it, not as a cheese board, but in a moment of necessity he must have grabbed one of his carpentry pencils and written down some quotes for timber he was ordering upon the top of the board.

The numbers in his neat hand, the divided line and the total.

And, perhaps in an afterthought as he looked at the quote, he had written in his flowing running writing, 'This cheese board is something.'

I laughed, then stopped and almost cried. He hadn't thrown it away. I sat holding it for some time, thinking of my father.

A LETTER TO MY DAUGHTER

The year before my daughter finished high school, she went on a Year 11 retreat, a time of reflection. The girls were given a letter written to them by their parents that they would read and reflect upon. This is the letter my daughter received from her father.

Dear Stella,

Hello, this is your father. I like nothing more than eating, gargling on my lolly water, thinking that perhaps Dean Martin was the most influential human since Plato and wearing rather fetching undergarments on my verandah at night.

Bad Humour Attempt Number 1.

If you think reading these sorts of letters is hard then try writing them. It goes without saying that I love you and that you are important to me.

That is why I often yell at you and behave like a grumpy arse.

But just how much you mean to me and how often I think of you I can't really put into words. It can't be quantified. You and your big brother are the most precious things in my life. And you are unquantifiable. That is what love means, I suppose. Or one of the things it means.

You are smart and funny and write quite beautifully.

You sometimes tell very good knock-knock jokes and sometimes very poor ones.

You remind me a lot of your mother but sometimes of me.

But most of all, Stelly, you are your own person and that is something that is about as fine as a person could be.

You won't always be happy. And that is okay, you know, because life is a mixed bag. You know that, we all know that in our family. You've had to say goodbye to a lot of people.

I was so proud of you when you went to Nanna's funeral. So proud.

And I can tell you this, you have lived through so much in your life so far, more than most kids your age should need to, but you are, if I could say, a fair sort of human being.

When you were born, your mum and I looked at you and you didn't do anything much.

Mum looked at you and said that you didn't have her mouth.

Then you let out a cry.

And your mum said, 'Well there, she has!'

We laughed and the doctor and the nurse laughed.

You never stopped giving us joy and happiness.

(Just had to demonstrate how much joy and happiness you evoke in me.)

Well, Stella, the fact that someone as wonderful as your mother loved you and was so proud of you and the fact

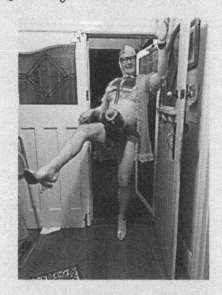

that someone as irascible as me is made a bit better and more complete by your presence in this world should hopefully tell you how much you mean.

Once when we went down to Barwon Heads and stayed at a house when I was working you hid from me.

To say I began to panic is an understatement. I went off my blob.

I was shouting and then yelling and then screaming your name. A very bad Marlon Brando.

And I felt a fear that I can't quite describe. Awful.

I ran into one of the bedrooms and for some reason got on the floor and looked under the bed.

And there you were. Smiling.

You were a frigging toddler. Smiling at me. Laughing.

I just want you to know that I can still remember holding you in my arms and feeling your body bubbling with laughter.

Cow for frightening me shitless, but it still makes me smile.

And I will never forget you holding my hand
during that flight to Japan when the turbulence
struck.

Stella Marion Lawson McInnes. You are glorious,
this world is a lovely place to be – it must be
because it has you in it.

All my love, Stelly,

your father.

Oh okay. He's not your father. But if he was he
would say 'The force is strong in you'.

And he would be grumpy and bad-tempered and
yell at you about your room. And fret about you,

worry and hope and wonder and <u>love</u> you. That is
what fathers do. Especially with someone like you.
And then he would point at you and your neck
would start to twitch and then your mouth would
go weird, and you'd start to choke. And he'd stop.
And then he'd yell at you about your room. And
then he'd jump in some star fighter to go and blow
up some planet and live out a cornball soap opera
set in space. So, no, better stick with this guy. Me.
Your father.

And even though Humphrey B Bear may never be
the same again, he knows I love you.

XXXXXXXXXXXXXX

2

BY HUMPYBONG CREEK

The things you think about in bed on a Sunday morning in late January. I was thinking of the small pyramid by Humpybong Creek in Redcliffe, and of fathers.

The pyramid was a monument of bluestone and wood to mark the establishment and construction of the Redcliffe Police Citizens Youth Club and to thank the people who'd raised money to have the hall built. The small pyramid seemed quite grand to me, especially when contrasted with the building it celebrated: a square fibro and besser-block hall. The hall wasn't a place I frequented much, but I passed it often enough when I went for a walk along the creek down to the shops. It was a hall where indoor sports took place, which were of little interest to me as I concerned myself mostly with outdoor pursuits such as cricket, rugby and tennis.

A few quiet kids I knew of from school played 'indoor sports', such as badminton, and a collection of even odder kids seemed to indulge in pastimes like gymnastics that were also conducted inside the hall.

These 'indoories' were boys who, for no seeming reason, would walk on their hands when they wanted to impress people. Like a boy with different coloured eyes who would wait in line at the tuckshop swaying to and fro on his hands and then rolling over onto his feet to stand upright with his face bright red and his different coloured eyes bulging like ping-pong balls in his bullet-shaped head.

I only entered the hall three times. Once on a supremely mortifying rainy Saturday when for some reason my mother had enrolled me into a holiday 'beginners gymnastic course' which only confirmed my prejudices about indoor sports. Especially as one of the tuckshop hand-walkers was helping teach people how to do somersaults and cartwheels.

The second time was when my father took me to see a fundraising event, a night of amateur boxing, for the Police Citizens Youth Club. The night was rather dubiously titled 'A Father and Son Glove Night'. Why he decided to take me was a slight mystery; although he had been a very handy boxer himself in his army days, to my knowledge he had never shown an inclination to attend boxing matches. And while I sat and watched like almost everybody else when a big boxing bout was broadcast on the telly, it was only when it was 'live via satellite' with someone like Muhammad Ali.

The impetus for the father–son boxing night could have been because the weekend prior I went off to a birthday fancy dress party as the TV character Aunty Jack, a cross-dressing creation of the comedian Grahame Bond. My costume consisted of a large-bosomed blouse, a boxing glove on one hand, spectacles, a heavy black moustache and a pair of high-cut football boots.

My father was driving one of his trucks home just as I was heading off and I caught his attention by waving my golden boxing glove at him. When he worked out who I was, he nearly drove through a neighbour's fence.

Perhaps it was the mixture of twin-set, footy boots and boxing glove that had got my father thinking that a local night of the noble gentlemen's sport of fisticuffs might be the go. Whatever the reason, my father and I set out along Humpybong Creek to the hall. I whined that I hoped there weren't any toads out. My father told me not to worry about bloody toads.

This I thought slightly odd because whenever one hopped into our house from the garden it was my mother who had to deal with the intruder.

My father told me to think about the soft drink and choccy bar that was on offer at intermission as part of the father–son night. I thought that sounded like a fair enough deal and then asked him if the police ran the centre.

'Sort of, there's always a walloper there, but it's something for everybody to use. Good places, although the bloke who set them up was a crook.'

I asked my old man why a crook would work with the police.

He laughed. 'Let's just say that there's a few fellas in the police who help themselves to things they shouldn't. Like Frank Bischof, he's the bloke whose idea these clubs were.'

Bischof, the Queensland police commissioner who had overseen the growth of Police Citizens Youth Clubs around the state, was also a mad gambler who left his position under a cloud of accusation and suspicion.

My father laughed to himself. 'You know the bugger was bent because he was Father of the Year, and he didn't have any children. Go work that out. Complete rorter.' If he was going to say anything else on the matter, he didn't get very far, for he suddenly stopped, jumped sideways a little and bellowed, 'Christ alive, watch that toad.'

I shrieked, he yelled and we ran around a swollen cane toad glaring dumbly on the path in front of us.

We made it to the hall with no more mishaps, and I asked if we might see Muhammad Ali tonight.

'Probably not, son, but I tell you what, we'll see somebody,' and we entered after my father had chatted to some of the other fathers he knew. I said hello to a couple of kids I recognised from school and football and then we went inside for a night of watching people of various ability try and belt each other.

My dad was right, there wasn't much danger of seeing Muhammad Ali, but there were other pugilistic identities battling it out in the ring: a skinny baker from Clontarf who was introduced as 'Battling Baker' and went all right even though he made odd sounds when he swung his fists. There was also the brother of the hand-walker from the tuckshop line. He got knocked into next week for most of his bout until he swung wildly and knocked out his albino opponent.

He celebrated with a handstand and my father growled, 'Showboat.'

'Too right,' echoed a few other fathers.

One boy in the audience I knew from school, a would-be tough who would say 'You wanna make something out of it?' when he pushed in front in bus lines, gasped and then cried when a boxer's eye was opened up and blood spurted out. His dad told him to shush, but when the boxer was being treated by his corner men the boy whimpered, 'I want to go home,' and so his father left in a huff with the would-be tough following.

'Can I get my Chokito?' he asked his dad. A Chokito was a caramel choc wafer, an exotic choice of chocolate bar, especially for a would-be school tough, and I felt some sort of retribution by fate when his father snapped back, 'No bloody Chokitos for sooks like you.'

As the would-be tough passed by, another boy from school said loudly, 'You want to make something out of it?', which made the boy cry more and his father crankier.

When intermission came I grabbed my can of Fanta and a Polly Waffle and sat with a couple of other boys around the pyramid while our fathers muttered about the fighters.

All the Redcliffe fighters won their bouts except for one, a kid not much older than me. After his fight, he sat not far from me with his bottom lip swollen to the size of a life raft and an eye closed, his collar turned up and his long hair carefully brushed. He was trying not to cry.

His dad asked him why he didn't go and get a drink.

The boy said he didn't deserve it.

His father shrugged and said, 'Suit yourself.'

All the time people laughed and roared at two little boys, barely bigger than their boxing gloves, swinging madly at each other. I looked at my father and saw him looking at the boy with the swollen lip.

After the fight people threw coins into the ring, and the little boys tried to pick up the ten- and twenty-cent pieces with their gloves still on.

The crowd roared and threw more money in the ring. After that 'bout' a loud man with a big gut thanked us all for coming, especially the fathers because he knew how busy they all were but it was good to bring along their sons just so they could see how we boys might know how to handle ourselves. Outside the hall, as people milled around, I mooched not far from the pyramid, my father standing with a group of other men, but looking at me for a long time.

It was an odd night and one that hung around some-where in my mind, which is probably why I remembered it that morning when I thought of the pyramid.

Just why I thought of that pyramid when I woke that morning after all those years can probably be explained by the fact that the previous night my children and I had watched Steven Spielberg's *Jaws*, the 1975 movie about the great white shark that terrorises a small coastal town.

There is something elementally thrilling about *Jaws* even though the mechanical shark almost has a street-parade-float-from-Warana air about it. Despite this, or maybe because of it, it seems that the movie is on a rotating list of perennial favourites to watch with my children, especially when we decide to have fish and chips in front of the telly.

And so, I woke and thought of the third time I went inside that hall.

It was to see a great white shark and a feral from the suburbs of the seventies, a man named Vic.

Vic Hislop used to exhibit great white sharks he'd caught out in the waters of Moreton Bay. The Brisbane paper *Sunday Sun* called him 'Brisbane's own Shark Hunter'. To my knowledge he only recently closed a museum in Hervey Bay based around him and his conquests of the great predatory fish. I first saw him a couple of years after the father–son glove night, when I was twelve and he was standing outside the hall, marshalling the crowds with a handlebar moustache, stubbies shorts and thin arms.

Vic mightn't have looked like a shark hunter from the movies but he'd killed heaps and stuck them in glass containers, where they looked milky and slightly off.

Fifty cents to see the great white shark. To see Jaws.

You walked into the hall, the home of the 'indoories' and their strange pastimes, and there on the basketball court, in place of the beam the gymnasts used, was a huge glass box filled with a huge fish, the head of the food chain.

When it comes to big fish pickled in formalin, Vic's effort took the cake. It had a distinctly homemade feel about it; in fact, I would go so far as to say it was the stuffing and preserving equivalent of my scone-cutter.

Not quite right, but still impressive.

It seemed odd that something so massive could have been vanquished by Vic, for he seemed very tiny as he talked to people who filed past to see his milky trophy.

'Why do it?' somebody asked him.

'For protection – would you want that thing out there? What would it do to us, to our kids? Eh?' he said.

There were some mutters of agreement and Vic nodded and put his hands on his hips.

'He's like the bloke from *Jaws*; the policeman,' said a young father to his son. 'It's what you do when you're a dad – protect people.'

The father was a large cream bun of a man as pasty and healthy-looking as the big fish in the tank. Nevertheless, he spoke again as he patted his kid's head with a big soggy paw, 'Fathers protect the ones they love.'

I was standing by that little pyramid looking at the podgy father and the shark hunter Vic, both evoking characters from *Jaws* as examples of what it meant to be a father. I remembered thinking then, as I did in my bed that late January morning, that they didn't look anything like Roy Scheider, who played Chief Brody in *Jaws*, the lean, tanned man with the slickback hair and aviator sunnies. The one who said, 'You're gonna need a bigger boat.'

He was a popular character in our house was Chief Brody, my daughter even dressing up as him on a school 'movie dress-up day' for some charity event.

I remembered reading that Roy Scheider had been a very good boxer, reaching the finals of the Golden Gloves competition in New York, before he became an actor. Then I remembered the father–son glove night. I remembered my old man's words about Frank Bischof, the brains behind the besser-block hall and the Father of the Year who wasn't even a father.

From another pigeonhole in my brain I picked up a truly minute piece of trivia: in the sequel to *Jaws*, imaginatively titled *Jaws 2*, there was a scene set in Chief Brody's office. This was before another large Warana-parade shark began prowling the waters off Amity and eating waterskiers and helicopters.

Brody was in his office talking to some citizen who was complaining about a neighbour's dancing at night and the two walked past a table with Chief Brody's Father of the Year award. Or something like it.

The cream bun dad and Vic the shark hunter wouldn't be the first, and certainly wouldn't be the last, people to evoke templates of fatherhood from popular culture.

The thing was, I realised as I scratched myself in bed, it was a pretty far stretch, perhaps nobly ambitious, to make a correlation between a lean, tanned Roy Scheider and his battles with a Warana shark and some fat bloke who couldn't see past his gut and would get a stitch just thinking about casting a line in the water, or even Vic who knew a little bit about fishing and protecting people in a suitably patriarchal manner.

In my early youth, there was a plethora of make-believe fathers to keep a mind busy on what being a father was supposed to be like, and many weren't that far from Roy and the Warana shark. Especially from the world of afternoon television. A host of shows dealt with young boys who, for whatever reason, were marooned in some frontier wilderness with a half-wild animal they had befriended and a father who was nearly always in some sort of khaki uniform, just like Roy.

Flipper was about a friendly dolphin who made some odd grating sounds by way of communication. *Skippy the Bush Kangaroo* was an Australian variant on the theme and had a porky little boy basically talking to himself a lot and getting yelled at by his father.

Gentle Ben was about a large friendly black bear in the Everglades who befriended a young boy and his ranger father. There was also a mother character who was relegated mostly to the kitchen. I think she got as far as the verandah in one episode but mostly she was housebound, as if she was more of a maid than a maternal figure.

Gentle Ben had the most bizarre opening credits, with the boy hero, his dad and the bear on a swamp boat, a shallow-bottomed punt with a huge mounted engine or fan at the back, which zoomed along the waters of the Florida Everglades.

The bear was chained to the boat and looked petrified even though it had probably been given a sedative, but not as terrified as the father, who was driving the boat and stared steadfastly ahead as if his sedatives were working a little too well, better than the bear's.

It didn't matter that the bear used in the show had had most of its teeth removed and had been declawed, a bear was a bear, especially on a fast-moving boat.

The *Flipper* father was a marine park ranger and was a little more laid-back and demure than his zonked-bear counterpart. He looked like a walking Ken doll and smiled a lot, as if a large marine mammal was a lot easier to be around than a large predatory bear.

But the khaki animal father closest to my own father was from *Skippy*. He was a grumpier sort of character and always had the air of having better things to be doing than hanging out with his son or a kangaroo. He even had an office like my father's and he would often disappear into it with a growled warning. 'Now be quiet, I've got work to do.' It was almost as if it wasn't too far of a stretch to have him saying other Dad things, like 'Are you going to make me get up out of my chair?' or 'Turn it down, you droob.'

My own father, though never in khaki, was a lot like this, almost as if we kids were an irritant to be put up with as he prowled around the house or 'Dadded around', as my mother put it, looking for things to fix up, pull down or burn.

It was fine by me, as if all I needed to know was that my father was around somewhere to step in when things might get a bit heated. That he'd be the one who'd come to the beach when you'd stayed past a set time, and mostly then it was just to check if things were okay, casually muttering: 'You right?'

My father's relationship with animals was also a little reminiscent of the khaki fathers because on these programs the animals were a kid thing and the khaki fathers only stepped in at the end to either tidy things up or give a pat on the head after the adventure had sorted itself out.

The sedated father from *Gentle Ben* never really did anything that I could remember, while laid-back *Flipper* father just smiled a lot and nodded. The *Skippy* dad would occasionally tell the kangaroo to 'Clear off, will you, Skippy,' which was the closest thing to what my father would say to our dogs. 'Get down, you bloody thing' or 'Who's a lovely boy, eh?' And he would scratch their tummies or give them a big bear hug not unlike the ones he would deliver to his children.

His other animal interactions were volcanic in a totally mundane everyday manner: he sat on the cat at dinner once and he leapt up so fast in reaction that he seemed to have been shot from a cannon. The cat, named Barney, was never quite right after that incident.

The only thing my old man said in sympathy as poor Barney staggered around bumping into various objects was, 'Lucky I didn't fart, or worse, that would have been the end of him.'

There was also the afternoon after a barbecue when my father, who was cuddling Sam, a blue heeler cross, came up with an idea about seeing if Sam would like to go down a slippery slide into the pool.

Nobody said anything for a moment. We were lolling about in the above-ground pool and Dad's eye had obviously been caught by the nearby slippery slide that was awaiting a trip to the dump. We all knew that Sam liked jumping in the pool to follow a ball or paddle about with us, but that was usually under his own steam. My father reckoned that, since the dog liked to jump into the pool occasionally, perhaps he'd like a slide into the pool.

There was a chorus of shouting and protesting that of course Sam wouldn't. My father cuddled him, and then said aloud, 'Who's to know?'

'No, Dad!' yelled my sister Corby.

'That Skippy drove a boat, you know, and that bloody bear went in the water the other day and you don't reckon Sammy would handle the slide?'

'That's only on the telly,' I said.

My father jiggled the dog and put him down. 'Sorry, Sam, overruled, but between you and me, I'd rate you above the bear.'

The dog promptly barked and jumped into the pool, my father held his hands out in mock despair, and went about the business of 'Dadding around'.

'Dad, you shouldn't muck around so much,' my sister Corby said. 'He,' she pointed to me, 'doesn't understand.'

I thought that a bit stiff but perhaps accurate.

I noticed other patriarchal figures on the television were different to the khaki fathers and seemed to be full of gravitas and common sense, ready with a steady reply that would put whatever drama had happened into perspective.

Fred MacMurray from the seemingly never-ending *My Three Sons* – who I think was a template for the pipe-smoking father from my Woolies portrait – exuded a country club composure when he sorted out whichever one of his three sons' problems had frothed up in any given episode.

Ironically, when he was a very old man, Fred MacMurray, the pipe-smoking pretend father from *My Three Sons*, sat watching a televised concert with his wife June Haver and she noticed that MacMurray's eyes were full of tears as he watched the solo violinist.

He told her he remembered how his father, a classical violinist, had rehearsed this same piece of music as MacMurray had played at his feet as a young boy.

His father had died not long after.

'I miss him,' said MacMurray. 'I miss being his son. I didn't really know what being a father was.'

It was the only time that June Haver could remember her husband talking about his father.

He knew enough, however, to be one of the most successful pretend TV fathers.

There was a story where one of his sons, Robbie, discovered that an interest in golf would perhaps curry favour with his dad, who was getting cranky with the boy for forgetting to pass on important phone messages.

When they enter a father–son golf tournament, Robbie starts to worry because his friends tell him that sooner or later it will all come to grief because all dads want to win. When it doesn't work out, they tell him, then you'll see just how much your father hates you.

Fred the pipe-smoker and Robbie do okay until Robbie chokes and four-putts a hole and then runs off.

He eventually comes home and is told to go see Fred the pipe-smoker upstairs. Fred, who's contemplating his pipe, tells Robbie how disappointed he is in him. Robbie blubs about the golf and having let his dad down and then Fred the pipe-smoker says he's not disappointed about the golf but that Robbie forgot to pass on another phone message.

Fred finishes filling his pipe and Robbie vows never to forget a phone message again.

That's it. The end.

My father harrumphed. 'That fella with the pipe wears a wig.'

He was talking about Fred.

'Dad,' one of my sisters said, 'would you be like that about golf?'

'What's that?'

'If one of us stuffed up golf. Or forgot a message.'

'Don't play golf, love,' said my father. 'Don't really care.'

'What if one of us forgot a message?'

'If you don't get a message that you're meant to get, you're going to get upset. That's fair enough, isn't it?'

'Yeah, but what about the golf?'

'I don't play bloody golf.'

'What if you did and we were playing golf together and we stuffed it up?'

My father was cuddling our dog. 'Christ almighty, it's not about the golf. Didn't you watch that claptrap?'

'Yes,' said my mother, 'we all did.' Then she looked at him and smiled. 'What would you do?'

'I'd take off my wig, give the pipe a miss and give that sook Robbie a big cuddle.'

He cuddled our dog. Then he whispered in Sam's ears, 'You sure you don't want to go down a slippery slide into the pool?'

●

Lying in my bed that late January morning I remembered how we had all shouted at my father again and then laughed. I liked that he wasn't at all like the TV fathers.

What my children thought of make-believe fathers in relation to me and my fathering, though, could be quite a sobering experience.

I have in my study a portrait of myself drawn by my son when he was a young boy. I don't have a pipe; instead, inside a gold-painted frame decorated with bits of pasta, is a goofy-looking figure with a big dopey smile.

'My dad' is written in a teacher's hand. Not that flattering but I kind of like it very much.

It didn't get much better when he was older. As one Father's Day approached, he was given a class assignment to draw what cartoon character your dad would be.

Mostly, according to his teacher, the kids picked Mufasa from the Disney movie *The Lion King*. Mufasa was the lion with a big voice and was incredibly courageous and kingly in the jungle. Noble and wise and adored by all, ready to put his life on the line to protect his son Simba in the face of a wildebeest stampede. A real Roy Scheider dad. If you'd have closed your eyes when watching the film, it might almost have seemed as if Mufasa was dressed in khaki.

There was a Homer Simpson that the teacher laughed about because the father in question was a super-fit triathlon competitor; and two Darth Vaders, who were both dentists.

'Makes you think, doesn't it?' she said quietly.

I couldn't help myself. 'Am I a Mufasa?'

'Ah yes, you. Well, you'll have to find out on Father's Day, won't you?'

And she laughed a little.

I was intrigued. I don't deny that the first time I saw *The Lion King* I thought it was fairly trite. The kids liked it but all those jock-like lions were pretty boring. Still, I'd have a crack at a wildebeest stampede if needed.

On the Father's Day in question, after my daughter had given me a burnt bit of toast and one of her dolls as a present and I had said thank you, I started to open my son's card.

I was about to attempt my best impression of James Earl Jones, the actor who voiced Mufasa, when I stopped and stared at the card.

I didn't even crack Homer or Darth Vader.

My son smiled at me rather sweetly and looked back to the card he had made.

'I love you dad' written in Clem's primary-school handwriting, under an image of the cartoon character who best represented me.

Foghorn Leghorn.

A *Looney Tunes* favourite. A big heavy-bottomed, large-voiced, loud and obnoxious barnyard rooster who had a penchant for mischief.

'Foghorn Leghorn?' I said.

'The big chook,' my son said.

'Big chookie,' said my daughter.

I was dumb enough to ask, 'Why no Mufasa?'

My son's smile half disappeared and then he said, 'Mufasa's sort of boring . . . and Foghorn the big chook is like you.'

I stared.

'He's funny, he never shuts up when he starts to tell a story, like Mum says about you.'

I looked at my wife who was trying not to drown laughing while drinking a coffee.

'And he laughs at his own jokes, just like you, and he always yells funny things.'

He smiled.

'I love Foghorn. I love you!'

I said in my best Foghorn Texas drawl, 'Ah say a say, come up here, boy!' and I gave him a cuddle.

And he gave me a cuddle and his sister jumped up and hugged my legs and said, 'Big chookie.'

•

My daughter was responsible for another trip to the make-believe father experience years later when she came home from her part-time job one night to find me watching *Taken* on free-to-air television.

It was another of those films which seemed to be on a high rotation screening. For anyone who isn't familiar with it, it can best be described as a middle-aged man's adventure fantasy. Liam Neeson, with badly dyed hair and an awkward flat-footed walk, beats up and dispatches men half his age and twice his size as he tries to rescue his abducted daughter.

In a famous scene from the film he is talking down a phone line to one of his daughter's abductors and he says he has a particular set of skills that he will use on them, the kidnappers, and he will kill them.

Taken is on TV so much that watching it has become something of a tradition, not quite *Jaws* but getting up there.

My daughter walked into the living room after grabbing some fruit from the fridge.

'Hey, it's old Bunnings himself.'

In the Bunnings hardware store down the beach is a store worker who is the spitting image of Liam Neeson. Even down to the way he dips his head when he smiles and walks. So much so, in fact, that people sometimes stop to have a selfie with him in his red shirt and apron and crinkled Neeson grin.

'Yep, old Bunnings is beating up Albanians again,' I said.

She bit into a peach. 'Would you do that for me, Dad?'

'What?' I asked.

'Would you fight in that sped-up way and dye your hair to rescue me if I got abducted?'

'Christ alive, don't say that! Why would you say that?' I shrieked.

She laughed.

'Come on, would you run around like that and use your particular set of skills to save me?'

'Stop it.'

'Well, it doesn't have to be me getting abducted then — what if someone took my seat on the train? Or someone pushed in front of me at a shop. Or took my coffee?'

I looked at her.

'I'd have a crack,' I managed.

She burst out laughing.

'With your particular set of skills!' she said.

I turned back to the TV as Liam was about to belt somebody and was measuring up his chances of getting to the door and then finding something else to quilt another large Albanian.

He was very precise and sure of himself. Him with his particular set of skills. Him with his name of Bryan. Him with his hair.

The penny dropped.

'Jesus, he's like a bloody manual arts teacher belting Albanians with scone-cutters!'

And then he did in fact belt an Albanian with a utensil which seemed to have been produced in a manual arts class.

My daughter laughed again. 'Random dad strikes again.'

I gave her a brief description of the characteristics of the manual arts teachers of my youth and their similarities to Liam Neeson's character Bryan in *Taken*.

She nodded, took another bite of her peach and said, 'Well, he does work at Bunnings.'

She bent down and gave me a peachy kiss on my head. 'Thanks for saying you'd have a crack.'

These days, when she asks me if I could give her a lift to a station or drop over a book or some little favour, she says, 'Hey, I need your particular skills, Dad,' and I smile.

Bryan the manual arts teacher from *Taken* would certainly be some person's idea of a Father of the Year and I like to think that the cream bun dad might have the boxed set of the series. It'd be right up his alley.

•

It seemed Father of the Year awards were just as pointless and as distant as make-believe fathers, even if a childless police commissioner who was an inveterate gambler was a rather exotic Queensland example of stretching things a bit.

Father of the Year awards had their beginnings in America.

In America, Father's Day had its own National Father's Day Council which gave awards to those who were deemed to have made a contribution to the national life by their professional achievements and also their family commitments. When Charles Lloyd Jones, the head of the Australian department store and retailing empire David Jones, visited America in 1957 he attended a Father's Day lunch and was so impressed that he helped create an Australian Father's Day Council and soon an Australian award was being handed out.

The fact that it was a major retailer who began the awards and popularised the concept of Father's Day in Australia isn't lost on the more skeptical, for the commercial benefits of creating and fostering another 'event' in the social calendar make some sense.

The very nature of the award meant that the winners had to be of enough note to be widely recognised in the general community and that their achievements had to come under the idea of nation-building, to light the way for other fathers who operated on a much smaller scale.

Neither the cream bun father or Vic the shark hunter ever had much of a chance of coming under that banner of nation-building do-gooders and I thought, there in my bed that January morning, nor would my father. True, he had served throughout the Second World War and had started his own business building houses and running a hire firm with articles such as homemade trestle tables that kneecapped people when they occasionally collapsed. He'd also stood for public office though he'd come up short. And even though he involved himself in service clubs and community organisations, he was still a bloke who wore striped t-shirts, stubbies shorts and work boots, and drove in a collection of loud and barely functioning vehicles.

I doubted any Father of the Year would hare around in the Canny Buy. And as far as my father's pursuits in science were concerned he was a great advocate of kerosene as a 'fire aid'. He kept some in a water pistol near the barbie and incinerator. 'Just shoot a small stream out, son,' he instructed my brother. 'Just to juice up the flame.'

His thinking was that the controlled 'flame-inspirer' would help things along, and he handled the orange Luger as a scientist might a microscope.

In the hands of us kids, the flame-inspirer was almost a lethal weapon and he would loudly declare we had no bloody idea how to use the thing. It was placed out of reach from our ignorant hands, in a box tied to a frangipani tree, to be used only by the 'people who knew how to handle it'.

He would occasionally point the plastic Luger at the barbie and say in a very bad war movie accent, 'Ve haff vays of makink you talk!'

And then he would roar when a flame erupted.

As the barbecue would often smoke uncontrollably, he would try to disperse the smoke through a squirt of the plastic Luger, achieving only a kerosene marinade on whatever was cooking on the plate. 'Napalm burgers with the lot,' he declared on one occasion along with a fried camp pie sandwich, which he assured us would be 'A taste of what helped win the war'. It should have been donated to the CSIRO as a deadly weapon.

So, no, not even a man like my father could hope to achieve the lofty heights of Father of the Year; that was the realm of businessmen, scientists, legal identities and politicians, with the odd sporting champion thrown in for populist appeal.

The organisers of the national award made sure that any other police commissioners who were given the title Father of the Year were at least men who had children.

Even so, some of the choices amongst the scientific, captains of industry and other noteworthies seemed to be out of the average man's orbit and some carried a fair bit of baggage and had the hint of political convenience.

Billy McMahon, who was one of the more ridiculous people to be the Prime Minister of Australia, was anointed as a Father of the Year during his rather brief and unspectacular tenure. 'They gave it to the poor little bugger because he had nothing else going for him – those kids of his are about the only good things he ever produced,' was my father's verdict. While the choice of one of the truly alcohol-affected public figures in Australia, the vice-regal booze hound Sir John Kerr, simply stunned everybody.

'That,' muttered my father, 'is going to end in tears.'

As I got older and became a father myself, it seemed to me that the criteria became slightly more random. You still had scientists like Graeme Clark, who developed the cochlear ear implant, and military heroes like the Victoria Cross winner Ben Roberts-Smith, who followed the pattern of men like the former war hero and diplomat Sir Arthur Roden Cutler, VC, and the ophthalmologist Sir Norman Gregg.

But then it seemed enough if your son was a grand slam winner and all-round good bloke and you had nine children, as in the case of Pat Rafter's father Jim. My mother said that Pat must have got his pleasant nature from somewhere so why not give his dad a gong?

So many of the Fathers of the Year seemed quite old, men who were in their sixties and seventies, a group of rather crusty and clubby men like Dick Casey and Robert Menzies. The perennial prime minister and reminder of a distant Australia, Robert Menzies was awarded the Father of the Year in 1964 at the age of seventy, and he spoke not only of being a father but a grandfather, of how his being nominated was at first a surprise until he read the list of former winners and realised that all of them were his chums.

It was a club after all. Then, being Menzies, he spoke about how he was reminded of the Walter Scott novel *Ivanhoe*, a tale of old empire and English honour, where an archer's contest is to take place and an archer is asked to 'fire a twinkling willow wand' and he says in response, 'Well, my grandsire drew a stout bow at the Battle of Hastings and I hope not to dishonour his name.'

Menzies said that he hoped his grandsons might say the same of him, that R. G. Menzies drew a stout bow. That there was 'a continuity of race'. He was in part most likely speaking strongly about his own long-held views of

Anglo–Australia and its continuity of 'Britishness' but he went on to express a sentiment of what it means to be a parent, a father, through the passage of time.

'If we ever get to that deplorable state, Sir, in which we think we are here today and gone tomorrow and that nothing matters very much, there will be no continuity in our history and there won't be a Father of the Day in fifty years' time, a Father of the Year. And therefore, I feel that what you are doing is to contribute something to the sense of continuity, the sense of history which has produced in our veins and in our minds and in our hearts, the great causes in our lifetime of our survival and of our success.'

Menzies was to live for another fourteen years and it's scarcely possible that he could have imagined what Australia would become or how quickly it would change. A place where nobody really read Sir Walter Scott much anymore and where uncommitted loyalty to the idea of a shared British history increasingly waned. Or perhaps he did, and that was why he ruminated upon 'the continuity of race'. He certainly would never have comprehended at that time, in 1964, that fifty years later somebody from a then considered marginal sport like basketball would be deemed worthy to become a fellow Father of the Year, like Andrew Gaze. More probably he knew elementally that his 'time' was drawing to an end, but his children and their children's time was yet to come.

I remembered my father's face as he looked at the boy who was trying not to cry beside the pyramid outside the besser-block hall on the father–son glove night. I thought of Fred the pipe-smoker's boy Robbie from *My Three Sons*. Maybe that kid wanted to box because he thought his old man would like it. Back then, on that night, I couldn't understand why my father walked towards him, stopped and dropped his hand on the boy who was the only loser on the night. 'Hey, you,' my father had said to the boy. 'Well done, you, best effort of the night. Toughest fight. You'll get him next time, plenty of Chokitos to come.'

The boy looked up, shrugged his shoulders and then nodded his head. Then he laughed a little.

My father nodded and called me over to walk home with him.

We stopped on the path after a while and looked back at the besser-block hall.

'What you think of that lot, then?'

I said it was all right.

'You like dressing up a bit, do you? Mucking around. Like the other day?'

He was talking about me going off to the birthday party dressed as Aunty Jack.

I didn't say anything.

He looked down at me for a while and then said softly, 'Well, cabbage head, that's okay then. Not my cup of tea, but that's okay.'

He balled his big hand into a fist and gently bopped me on my head. 'I love you. You'll be all right.'

There was a plopping sound nearby and my father jumped a little.

'Christ alive, it's those bloody toads. Race you home.'

And we ran off, hopping and yelling along the banks of the creek to the lights of the street and then to home.

I lay in bed and remembered. How that boy who had lost had stood a bit taller after my old man had chatted to him. How long it had taken me to realise why my old man had stopped and chatted to him. How much I had liked him telling me it was okay to like different things to him, things that weren't his cup of tea.

And I remembered an old song from the long-ago 1970s sung by a group called Pilot. I first saw it on *Countdown* and it had been a bit of an earworm for me that month. The song was called 'January'. It was a catchy, whiny bit of mid-shelf glam pop which overcame the rather hapless nature of the band members. There was a deeply dodgy-looking bass player who my father had said looked like a nervous shoplifter, while he thought a nasally uncertain lead singer was at one point winsome and another point acting like a flick-knife-wielding baddy from the English cop show *The Sweeney*. 'He'll take him off to the clink before the song is through.'

For some reason I sang the song to myself while I was out fishing one night with my Alvey rod and reel in the New Year. Why? Well it was January, so the song seemed to suit the month we were in, especially when you think of how fallow a time January seems to be in terms of the rest of the year. It's a time where you drift through a backdrop of big sporting events or maybe spend a bit of time deciding which New Year resolutions to jettison, especially if you've unwisely made any in front of people, and otherwise you basically plan for the year ahead.

That song, 'January', is a catchy little thing, and it has lyrics that speak to a certain optimism about life and being a human being.

I may have been in a generous and indulgent frame of mind but I liked the idea of life being enough of an intoxicant to make somebody want to show the world what was up, to wake up to a new year and do more stuff.

75

It's a good feeling to take into a new year, for with the passing of each year a part of all of us knows we are a step or two closer to the end.

Perhaps that sense of time passing was made more acute because of that 'January' themed fishing trip with my Alvey rod and reel.

There are some things that make me think inevitably of Brisbane and two are an Alvey rod and reel. I was given a set years ago by my father, who never really had the patience for fishing. Anytime we had gone together he couldn't wait for it to be finished, sometimes kicking bait surreptitiously into the water or piling so much squid, pippies and prawns onto his hook it was as if he was providing some sort of buffet for the fish below. Or perhaps it was the time he had sat on a hook in a small boat we had hired and the chin-wobbling roar he emitted was so loud and his crouched rowing to get back into the shore and to aid was so frenetic and operatically funny it could never be topped.

Fishing wasn't really his cup of tea, but he had thought it might be something I would like. I carry the rod and reel with me wherever I travel in Australia.

The side-cast reel design has always been to me a mark of Queensland ingenuity, with its distinctive logo and an ever-lingering company tagline, 'The Alvey reel fills the Creel'. I doubt whether many people even know what a creel is these days: it's a wicker basket you carried your fish home in. It's a shame, but I suppose that's just time bouncing along.

It's such a lovely thing, that beautiful silver side-cast reel, making a sound so pure and purring when you sweep out a cast that you almost don't care whether you catch anything.

When it was announced that the Alvey family business would be closing down, orders flooded in to give a bit of a boost to the business, but the writing was on the wall.

The Alvey reels were simply made too well, they never let you down, and with the evolution of mass-produced, easily replaceable fishing tackle equipment flooding the market, quality came, it seems, at too high a price.

That Christmas, fuelled by a bit of sentimental longing, I had done my bit for an old friend and bought my son a side-cast reel and rod. The look on his face when he opened the badly wrapped present was bang on. He smiled and said slowly, 'An Alvey.'

We went fishing together.

I told him about the father–son glove night and, as I did, I thought how, even if it had nothing really to do with us, the phrase 'Well, my grandsire drew a stout bow at the

Battle of Hastings and I hope not to dishonour his name' had a sentimental feel about it that sort of hung around one's mind a bit. Of remembering fathers and grandfathers, of continuity.

Halfway through the night, and after the twentieth time I had half hummed and half sung 'January', my son said quietly, 'We should do this a bit more often, Dad. It's good.'

And it was. January, a time to look ahead, a time to wake up the world and a time to remember.

3

OTHER PEOPLE'S FATHERS, PART 1

*I*f there is a better place to have a beer than the North Bondi RSL then it would have to be pretty special. I'm sipping on a frothy as I stare at the postcard view before me and having a bit of a ruminate. The RSL opens onto the beach and before me is the whole of Bondi's crescent moon of sands, stretching to the Bondi Icebergs swimming pool and then beyond to the iconic Waverley Cemetery.

Beach-blown Sydney.

Tables of people fresh off the beach, damp and sandy, surround me; families, friends and tourists. A dreadlocked father sharing a fisherman's basket with his son. They're laughing. The father has taken a beach towel and made a makeshift cushion to give the chair some protection from the boy's wet board shorts.

The boy wriggles a bit and says, 'This is weird, I'm up so high, you made it so big, Dad.'

The father shrugs. 'I told you to take your boardies off. You can just sit there in wet dacks.'

'They're my best pants ever – I'm not taking them off.'

The father shrugs his shoulders again. 'Just sit still and eat your food. Go on, get stuck in.'

The boy picks up a chip and just before he puts it in his mouth he pokes at something in the plastic basket. 'What's this? This thing.' And he pops the chip in his mouth and chews.

'It's beautiful,' says the father. 'It's a sea scallop.'

The boy picks it up. Looks at his dad. He isn't sure but he's game. He takes a bite and makes a face. He must have hit the roe. His father watches him, trying not to laugh, before letting out a peal of giggles as his son shakes his head and smiles.

Not far from their table, walking slowly across the parquet dance floor, a big burly man with tradies' hands gently leads an older man to the view.

'Come on, Dad, this way, there's the view for you,' he says.

The man stands blankly. He is shaky, uncertain. Not well.

'Your beach, Dad,' says the burly man.

Then a young woman takes the old man's other hand and says, 'Your beach, yours and Nanna's. Where you met. You and Nanna.'

The old man opens his mouth a few times but says nothing.

'Your beach, Dad, where you met Mum for the first time. You met her in the water. She got stuck in a rip and you stayed with her. Her name was Patricia. Pat. You called her Pattie,' says his son.

The old man turns away from the beach and stands still on the dance floor. He looks up at the television. His burly son's big shoulders shudder a bit. 'Your beach, Dad.' After a few moments, he says to his daughter, 'I thought he might remember.'

His daughter reaches out, gently touching her father's shoulder. 'Let him watch the footy,' she says.

Her father looks at her and nods. They sit not far away from me at a table and the old man looks up at the television.

The daughter holds her burly father's hand.

The footy sides slugging it out are the Storm and the Roosters, a replay from the previous weekend. The old man is the only one watching the TV for it's too beautiful a day. Too beautiful a picture. The tide is going out on the beach and, even though it's the twenty-first century and Bondi is an international destination, the picture is clouded in the past, of an older Australia.

The art deco units on the headland, the pavilion and people on the sands dotting the beach like happy flies all speak of Max Dupain's black-and-white portraits.

I remember how my wife and I would always come to this RSL for a drink whenever we were in Sydney. Beaches make me think of her.

The first time I met her was in Bronte, another beach suburb further along. I opened the front door and there she was in the doorway waiting. She'd come to visit a housemate.

She wore Wayfarer sunglasses, a green dress and black boots. Behind her was her S Series Valiant. She flipped up her Wayfarers and smiled.

I think of that moment sitting here in this RSL so full of memories. The water is so blue and the day is so fine.

I remember when my kids were younger, about ten years before, when their mother had become sick a second time and we were staying in Sydney. How she had wanted to rest in bed a bit and I had brought the kids to this RSL. I had told them of how I had met their mother, of how we would come here. I bought them both Fire Engines, red flavoured schooners of soda water, and we had looked down on the beach. Then we had walked from Bondi to Clovelly, walking along the sandstone cliffs and stopping to swim at each beach along the way. At Bronte I was picked up and dumped. I staggered out and my kids laughed.

I told them how their mother and I had swum at Bronte Beach when we were first going out, how I had been dumped and when I had walked out of the surf, their mother had laughed in the same gut-busting way they had. Then I told them how she had bought Splice ice-blocks to make me feel better.

'Did it work?' my kids asked.

I nodded. It had.

My children smiled at me and I shrugged my shoulders. We went and bought Splices and sat giggling on the beach.

I look over to the old man watching the footy on the TV, and I feel very glad that I had told my children how I had met their mother, for they remember.

Sometimes when they have been in Sydney by themselves, they have rung or texted from the Bondi RSL just to say hello and tell me where they are, the place where 'you and Mum would go'.

Coming back from the food counter area are three kids and their father. He has a harried look but is in no hurry.

He walks slowly as two of the children are arguing over what they have on their plates.

'She's got more chips.'

'You've got a parma, Scott, you wanted a parma, a chicken parma, and that's the amount of chips you get with a parma. With fish you get more . . .'

'I got more chips, I got more chips!' says the girl with the fish.

'She's got better chips,' says Scott.

'The chips are the same. That's the chips you've got and that's the chips you'll eat. The chips are the chips,' says the father.

'She's got more.'

'Dylan's done it again, Dad,' says the girl with more chips.

The father looks down at his third child, the smallest of the three. The little boy has buried his face in his sauce bowl. A great dollop of sauce is on his nose. The kid is smiling at his father. 'Saucy,' says the little boy.

The father just stares at his son. After a while, he says, 'Indeed.'

Scott starts to protest about the chips and the father quietens him, 'The chips are the chips.'

And they go and sit at a table in the corner.

•

Earlier in the day, while we were shooting scenes in a TV drama about police investigations into gay hate crimes in the late 1980s, Noah Taylor was approached by a punter who told him what a big fan of his he was.

Noah said thank you.

The punter said, 'It's such a thrill; to meet Ben Mendelsohn.'

Noah nodded and said, 'Well, how would you feel if you met Noah Taylor?'

The punter looked confused and then apologised.

I laughed.

Later, during a scene where I was looking at a pretend dead body below, a jogger from the public stopped and said to me, 'You look like that bloke off the TV. That McInnes bloke.'

Then he laughed. 'Hey, you fat sod, didn't you used to be William McInnes?'

I said, 'I think I was.'

The jogger laughed and said sorry but he didn't think that I would mind a bit of ribbing.

I said, 'It's okay, no worries.'

Then he asked if he could take a selfie, his dad would like it, he said. 'Because he likes your books.'

We posed and he jogged off.

Noah Taylor smiled and said it must be a real skill to get mistaken for yourself. I nodded.

'Well at least you made his dad happy,' said Noah.

In the RSL I laugh to myself. I think about these people around me, about their fathers. There are experiences that we share, but there are also elements about other people's fathers which elude me.

The first other father I can remember was a man called Gordon, or Gordy as he was known in the neighbourhood. He was a tall, thin man with dark hair and dark horn-rimmed glasses. He had a wispy thin moustache and would wear a white singlet and black shorts. Once I saw him in an army uniform on a Thursday and thought him to be a soldier.

'Reservist,' sniffed my father. 'He's in the reserve.'

He had two daughters about my age who would come and play with me and two of my other mates in a big spare block at the bottom of a house that bordered our block. The grass was long and we'd pretend to be in a jungle, sometimes a hybrid of a Tarzan adventure and playing soldiers in a far-off place called Viet Nam. Although the real danger came from the odd cane toad or the clinging buds from the top of the stalks that seemed to stick to every part of your body if you brushed against them.

We were all busy ferreting among the grass when we heard someone calling out the girls' names.

It was Gordon.

As soon as the girls heard him they went still, hardly breathing.

He was coming closer.

'You in the grass? You in the grass!' he called. 'You know what you'll get, you know,' he yelled. I knew what was coming because I had seen him do it before: slowly take off his belt and roll it into a coil.

There were a few moments of quiet and then a cracking, snapping sound. He had taken off his belt and had doubled it around in a loop and was snapping the leather together.

'I'm going to get you.' He didn't have to yell now, for he was closer.

The eldest girl closed her eyes and the youngest started to cry.

I thought it terrifying. I started to move, to stand up, and the eldest girl whispered, 'Please don't.'

So, instead, I crouched ready to run. I felt like pissing myself when I heard the belt snap again and Gordon said, 'You know what you gonna get.'

He was very close. It seemed very quiet. The eldest girl began to stand very slowly. And then her sister followed.

The belt snapped again and I stood.

Gordon stood with his wispy mo, and funny little chest. Even though, like us, he was not much taller than the grass stalks, he was still a grown-up.

The two other boys ran off crouching in the grass.

Gordon looked at me.

'Lunch for the girls,' he said, the belt still coiled in his hands.

I didn't say anything. My leg trembled from a cramp after crouching.

His two daughters looked down and walked off. Gordon stood in front of me and slowly snapped the belt, not making much noise, a soft little clap.

'Lunch,' he said and turned and followed his daughters.

I watched them go. I had never seen him use the belt against them. I supposed he would have, but to him having them cower at the threat was enough.

Threats from fathers were common enough, but the girls' treatment was so odd and out of place from my own experience with my father that I never quite forgot how Gordon had looked.

It wasn't the last time I would see such behaviour. Another friend's father was a former first grade rugby league player, and an immense human being. He would sometimes shape up to punch or strike his son. My friend would flinch, even cringe, and his father would sniff and half laugh. As we grew older, I realised that my friend's father mostly did it in front of us, his son's mates. Perhaps a behavioural specialist could elaborate on why a father would behave in such a way, but I remember my own father's words when I spoke to him about Gordon and his belt. He looked around, trying to get a bead on my mother's whereabouts, so I knew that a blokey, man-to-man tone was about to be employed.

'Listen, sunshine, Gordon's a shit-kicker. He's got a job he doesn't like where people tell him what to do every minute of the day. He's a bully. He dresses himself up as a Thursday night soldier, but he's just full of piss and wind. He's scared, that why he snaps his belt.'

And then he poked me in the chest. 'You be nice to those girls when you can.'

A father can be a big man, a footy hero even, and still be full of piss and wind, full of fear for some reason and so he looks around to prove to somebody that he's not what he thinks he is: a weak man without much power.

The dreadful thing about people like Gordon and my friend's football hero dad was how they distorted one of the great growing-up experiences: learning that father threats can be an immensely enjoyable collection of nonsense.

Father threats were often issued by way of a mother, 'Just wait till your father gets home.' This was a double deal because you had to go through the agony of waiting for your old man to arrive, then there would be the 'chat' and then whatever would happen would happen. More often than not, just before the father's arrival the mother would say quietly, 'Well, we'll leave *it*,' (the incident that had necessitated the threat was always accentuated like this) 'between us – but you just be careful.'

And for a while you were.

I'm sure the last thing any father really wanted after a day at work was to have to come home and turn into Dirty Harry. I was watching my kids playing school sport once and another father, a quiet man, said suddenly that he hated having to be the bad cop when he finished work for the day. Another father nodded. 'The just-wait-till-your-father-gets-home syndrome, eh?'

The quiet man nodded, thought for a bit and then decided to add, 'Although in my case it's not "wait till your father gets home". I work from home.'

We digested the clarification and the other father tried to make things clear. 'How does that go for you, mate?'

The quiet man looked like he wished he hadn't said anything but also felt he should go on. 'I work as a researcher and my home office is in the cellar of the house. It's quiet there, no noise – so it's more like, "Just wait till your father finishes his business in the cellar".'

We thought for a bit. 'The more you think about it, that doesn't sound too good,' I said.

'I know,' said the quiet man. 'Like something Norman Bates would do. Or something from a Stephen King novel. My wife said it a couple of times when she was picking the kids up at school and I'm still getting funny looks at parent–teacher meetings.' He half smiled and went on, 'It's a little smirk they get and they say, "Oh, you're the father from the cellar."' He shook his head. 'Quite odd.'

Like father threats from a mother, threats coming directly from a father also implied some sort of awaiting doom. 'Do I have to get out of my chair?' or 'Do I have to stop the car?' were two of the most common tools in the father's kitbag.

These two activities, sitting in a chair after work, and driving, usually on a holiday road trip, were generally what fathers did a lot of when father threats were made. A father resting in his chair signified that the day's work was done and now Dad was relaxing, drawing stumps on the grown-up's day. The chair threat was almost nuclear if the chair was in front of the television and a father show, sports or news usually, was on. If a newspaper was also being held then it would be better for the target of the threat to simply head for the hills.

Whatever was going to happen when the father got out of his chair or stopped the car wasn't specified, but the threat was there. While my father was more of a 'Do I have to get out of my chair?' fellow, a friend of mine had a father who was mad for 'Do I have to stop the car?' As soon as the phrase was proclaimed by this dad, usually on a long trip, whatever nonsense or noise was going on in the back seat stopped.

Once though, my friend's brother, who was a curious lad, wanted to see what would happen if he didn't stop doing what was annoying his father.

'Right,' the father said and slowed the car and flicked the indicator. The ticking sounded like a bomb about to go off. My friend's brother went silent.

Perhaps, the kids thought, the father would flick the indicator off and then resume driving. He had done that once before. But no, he pulled the car into a carpark by the side of the road.

The worst thing had happened; the car had stopped. The children sat mute. The father sat and stared ahead.

'Do I have to turn off the engine?' he said.

My friend's brother then said, very softly, 'Sorry.'

After a few seconds of stony silence, the father nodded and said, 'All right, but next time, if I have to stop the car . . . and turn the engine off . . .' He let the threat hang in the air.

Doom had only just been avoided and for a while if my friend's brother was behaving in an annoying way he would be branded as the 'car stopper' by his siblings.

My friend said it took them years to work out that their father had no plan on how to punish them, but just kept setting the bar to their dreaded fate a little ahead of where he said it would be.

Years afterwards, she asked him at a family Christmas what would have happened after the car had stopped.

'Well, my dear, I really don't know. I was actually surprised that I got such good service out of using the car-stopping business as a threat. Used to think that there was a possibility of you lot being a bit slow, a bit dim.'

My friend's brother said a little too loudly, 'I knew nothing would have happened.'

The rest of his siblings, all with partners, husbands and wives and families of their own, screamed at the top of their lungs, 'Car stopper!'

Some fathers' threats made little sense. 'I'm going to take you around the block and drop you in the deep end' was a favourite of the father who was our junior football coach. It didn't mean anything of course, just a bit of colourful linguistic pyrotechnics from a more unreconstructed time. The footy coach was a kind and lovely man who did an amazing amount of charity work during his life but once, during a match, he become so enraged at my inability to hold onto the ball that at half-time he gave me a spray which included a father threat, 'You, you didn't come out right. You should have been knocked on the head – there's still time, you know!'

One of his sons whispered to me, 'Hey, Willy, welcome to the family, he says that to us all the time.'

As we ran back on for the second half the coach came over and patted me on the back. 'You're right, son, you know what I mean.'

'Don't drop the ball.'

'Good lad,' said the coach.

He then turned to my dad, who had come to watch the second half and who'd heard the coach's old-school blast to me.

'Sorry, Col, you know what I meant.'

'No worries, mate, not the first time it's been said.'

And I heard them laughing.

The first ball I went to take from the back of the ruck, I dropped stone cold. Amongst the groans from the sidelines, I heard my father yell, 'I'll get the bloody hammer.' More laughing and at the end of the game, even though I hadn't been that great, I got a hug from my father and a pat on the back from the coach.

These father threats were an example, I think, of a more operatic form of fatherly frustration, never taken seriously. A lesson in how language could give vent to emotion, lessen tension and make things normal. They were never the same as that latent threat of Gordon and his belt.

•

Sitting in the RSL at Bondi with the view makes me remember another body of water, other fathers, sunsets and mullets.

Sunsets are funny things. You know somewhere deep within you a sunset means you are nearer the end of your journey through life but yet a sunset is still a glorious wonder to quietly enjoy and celebrate.

A sunset on the Noosa River I saw recently was a beauty.

I just stopped, and watched.

Water patterns softly dancing in different directions, shrouding big elegant catamarans anchored in the deeper water and little tinnies with their owners silhouetted as they dangled lines.

In between the tinnies, fish jumped intermittently.

Below, on the river's edge, a family stood together watching the sky. They laughed and a man's voice sang out, 'Let's get a selfie for Nathan!' He tried to corral people, 'Come on. Come on, for Nathan.'

'Oh steady on, Dad,' said somebody.

'No, come on, let's show him the arvo.'

And arm in arm, they clustered together, smiling, raising their glasses to Nathan with the beautiful sky behind and I thought, how lovely to get a message like that, from people who loved you.

Good for Nathan, wherever he might be.

And then a gondola prowled by. Why not? Far from the canals of Venice, the gondolier wore a baseball cap instead of a broad-brimmed hat, with no guiding pole, just a lazy hand on a long tiller.

Noosa was a tourist town and someone had obviously come up with a cracking coin-turner, a romantic prowl around the Noosa waterways in a transplanted gondola.

Well, good luck to them, it might be wonderful.

And then the fish jumped again. The fish were mullet. I laughed, doubting mullet would jump around the beauties of old Venice.

And then I wondered why mullet jump. To see the sunset? I knew they jumped to avoid predators and that they also fill the back of their throat with air, enabling them to be more active in the water.

In the scheme of things, the humble mullet punches above its weight. A low-rent staple of fish and chipperies, it transcends the watery world by leaping into our vernacular although not in a particularly complimentary manner.

A few phrases come to mind, a rugby coach screaming at me once as I stood staring at a ball on the ground, 'It's no bloody use standing there like a stunned mullet, pick it up!'

Or as was used by occasional male grown-ups of my youth, like a father at a high school awards night who deemed it necessary to tell his family and others in a school assembly hall that he was leaving for the toilet, 'I'm off to back out a mullet.'

Or my father calling a referee at Corbett Park 'a mullet-headed fool' after a scrum decision against the Dolphins.

And of course that little leaping fishy cameo from the sunset also gives its name to one of the more questionable hairstyles we humans concocted. The mullet. Business at the front, party at the back.

Why call it a mullet?

There's lots of theories – that it was the style worn by Icelandic fisherman to keep their necks warm while fishing for sea mullet or that, like mullet in a fish and chip shop, it's cheap and basic. Perhaps it's best to treat the mullet hairstyle like a sunset: a startling, wondrous marvel of nature.

My father hated the hairstyle and would stare at me and growl, 'Why don't you get a proper bloody haircut? It looks like something's died on top of your head.'

I would have been about seventeen when I had the 'something has died on top of your head' hairstyle. When my son was of a similar age, he wanted to ask me for a favour.

He needed a note from me to help save Murray.

I asked who or what was Murray.

My son smiled at me.

'Is this some school thing? Are you doing some environmental project about the Murray River?'

My son laughed out loud and wiggled his hand, indicating that I was in the right subject area.

'Christ alive, what do you want me to do?' I snapped.

He told me Murray was his mullet. His was a little more ornate than mine had been and the deputy head at his school had told him to have it cut as it was not in keeping with the school's guidelines for student appearance.

When I was a seventeen-year-old with a mullet I had received a similar letter from school and had not approached my father, I had simply trudged off to have my head shorn.

I stared, a bit stupefied, at my son and asked again what he wanted me to do.

'Could you write a note saying I have to keep it? Just until the end of term?'

'What?' I said.

'It's just that we were wondering how long I could keep Murray and if I could hang on to him till the end of term that would be pretty good.'

'What would the note say?'

'That I need Murray for work – just until the end of term.'

'You'll never get away with it.'

'I have to try.'

I stared at him and then I laughed. 'I am not going to lie, I'll put in the note that you say you need to have the mullet –'

'Murray, Dad, he's got a name.'

'– you need to have Murray for work.'

'Thanks, Dad.'

I wrote the note and received an email from the deputy head, who was obviously an educator with a sense of humour. He would allow the hairstyle to be kept until the end of term, which was only a week away, but after 'the performance' a more appropriate haircut needed to be presented. At the end of the email the deputy wished my son 'all the best with the performance'.

'What's the performance? What does that mean?' I asked my boy.

'A modelling job,' said my son.

I stared.

'A fashion shoot,' he said.

'For what?' I asked.

'Didn't get that far, but the deputy head laughed a bit.'

It seemed my son and some of his mates had engaged in a 'Murray fund', pledges of monetary support if the mullet would remain intact until the end of term, which raised a bit of coin for a charity with which the school was associated. I made sure that when Murray had fulfilled his fundraising target, he disappeared from my son's melon.

I had never heard of a mullet hairstyle being called a Murray before, but I added it to my list of names for this particular hairstyle. The Toowoomba Top Hat, the Bundaberg Waterfall and one directed at me by a father of a girl I was about to take out on a date. She was from one of Brisbane's better suburbs and as I walked up the front stairs I heard him asking her, 'This bloke you're going out with, is he that boofhead with the ape drape? The boy from Redcliffe?'

There was a pause where my date must have nodded in the affirmative because I heard the father say: 'Redcliffe! Does the bugger walk upright?'

I knocked on the door and when he opened it I beat my chest and hooted a few times, nodded and did my best simian walk.

The father stared hard but I am pleased to note my date and her mother laughed.

He drew me aside and proffered one of the silliest father threats I think I ever heard.

'Listen, son, get back home at a reasonable hour, behave yourself or it's Krakatoa East of Java for you.'

If you are not familiar with the phrase nobody would blame you. It relates in part to the volcanic explosion on the Indonesian island of Krakatoa in 1883 which was so cataclysmic it obliterated most of the island.

In 1969 there was an American film released called *Krakatoa, East of Java* which was one of the first disaster films, a genre which would become popular in the 1970s. The film's title is geographically incorrect by 180 degrees, the island was actually west of Java but the producers believed East of Java made for a snappier title, although not necessarily a quality film. It was a bit of a howler by all accounts, but the title of the film earned itself a bit of mid-shelf linguistic legend by being a favoured father threat by a certain professional class of father in south-east Queensland. The sort of fellow who thought that the calling down of volcanic obliterating doom, though geographically inept, was going to pull into line an ape-drape boofhead from Redcliffe was obviously somebody who is more to be pitied than scolded. Still, he cared enough to have a crack — a Crack-atoa, in fact.

Sometimes catching fathers in a reflective frame of mind can be a little too revealing, especially at a charged social occasion. When I was an unemployed actor I landed a job stocking and restocking a bar at a wedding that would have passed as a coronation of some middle-ranking monarchy.

It was at the pointy end of the 1980s and there was a whiff of excess in the air. The reception was in a massive courtyard with harbour views, there were shoulder pads on shoulder pads, big hair for the women, bigger hair for some of the men and lots of pastels and bling.

It was very humid, as if a belting Sydney storm could break at any moment, and underneath the celebrative air was a feel of people going at things hard and fast.

Mai tais, Tom Collins, White Russians and champagne were being poured and swallowed at a suitably hectic and indulgent late-eighties pace. All the speeches had been made and were what one might expect: the couple were so happy that they could share their special day with the people they most loved and admired – their families. A few telegrams were read out and even more faxes. 'How 1990s is that! Faxes!' said the best man.

The reception was underway, a band that I recognised from television was playing, and the wedding party had dispersed to various sections of the courtyard.

Another bar worker told me that the father of the groom, whose house this was and who had basically bankrolled the wedding, was in the process of getting a divorce from his wife, the mother of the groom.

There was also a sniff that parts of the father's business empire were going down the gurgler and that whatever was left was being spent tonight.

While I was stocking tubs with ice and bottles of Stolichnaya vodka, I heard a voice call to me. It was the father of the groom, the one who had paid for the wedding.

'Give us a beer if you have one,' he said. 'And a glass, ice and a bottle of Stoli.'

I gave him what he had asked for and as he poured the vodka, a great peal of thunder broke above.

Some guests shrieked and some ran for cover under the marquees. The father stood still. The band said they might take a break for a bit, just to get the gear under cover.

The father took the glass of Stoli and swallowed it. Then he took the stubby of beer and said, 'There's a storm coming, that's for sure. A fucking deluge.'

As more people scurried past, he took a deep breath and sighed. 'I should never have had children, that much I do know.'

And as the drops began to fall he simply stood with his bottle of Stoli in the rain.

A young man came up to him, slapped him on the shoulder and said, 'Bit of rain won't ruin the wedding, Dad!'

And then he ran off laughing with a woman in a peach dress that looked like an inverted triangle.

The father stared after them. 'Should never have had them.'

I remembered how matter-of-factly he had said it and how I had laughed as he stood in the rain. But now sitting in the RSL overlooking Bondi Beach, sipping a beer after working on the television series about the gay hate murders of the late eighties, it doesn't strike me as that funny. How a father could wish away his children, his fatherhood. I sit and think of what the parents of the gay hate victims must have felt and gone through. What they still go through.

Of how their son, their child, was taken from them so violently. For most parents it is a thought so awful it can barely be imagined. Perhaps most fathers wipe the thought from their minds and they do their best to hold their child close.

•

Being a father, it strikes me in the RSL, is about coming to terms with change, and sometimes, if a society is fortunate, then change can mean an acceptance of growth.

Many years ago, I was invited to the family dinner of a girl with whom I was friendly. They must have thought I was a lot friendlier than I was because the television was turned off for the meal – a sign of deep significance to me, for the television in our house was seldom off.

The father and I stood and shook hands as I was introduced to him. He had been watching a television show called *Wild Kingdom* with his two younger children, a girl and a little boy. He went to turn the TV off but the little boy asked to watch a little bit more, just to see who won the fight. *Wild Kingdom* was about animals fighting or eating each other – which was a handy coincidence because the program was always shown around dinnertime. It was hosted by a man called Marlin Perkins and he would whine on about wildebeests, warthogs, lions and the like while families and the big cats would both tuck in.

Tonight, it was baboons. Their behaviour in the *Wild Kingdom* struck the father of the household as odd. Some new baboon was being chased off by the others because he wasn't from their tribe or whatever it was you call a group of baboons.

'Stupid animals. They're completely the same, look at them. Can't tell the difference. No wonder they stayed in the trees.' We watched them fight and then he turned the television off and we walked to the table.

'It's not like those monkeys are really different from each other. Not like us – we can tell who's different to us. Look at these Vietnamese people that are coming in here.' And he raised his eyebrows.

Nothing more was said about immigrants or dim-witted baboons and we settled down to a feast of rissoles, gravy and Rosella savoury rice.

We chewed like a collection of creatures from *Wild Kingdom* and he asked me, 'What do you want to do with your life?'

I managed to drag up an old cricketing analogy. 'I'm just seeing how it comes out of the hand at the moment.'

I don't think the father was impressed.

'Well, you don't want to wait too long, best to have a plan.'

My only thought was, I'm not that friendly with your daughter. 'What do you want to do with your life' had all the hallmarks of being sussed out as a potential permanent member of the dinner table. And if not that, then a guide to be used by a father of how his daughter is travelling along the road to womanhood.

I was going to be catalogued as one of her develop-mental mistakes perhaps: 'You remember that William?

He was hopeless. Nice enough but had no plan of attack on life . . . and remember how he played with the Rosella savoury rice? No, glad that one got away.'

Otherness comes in many forms; indeed, my mother was full of advice about the dangers of otherness – never trust people who had no lobes to their ears or if they had webbing between their toes or if their eyes were too close together. My father never liked people with beards and was wary of left-handers.

But the most obvious idea of otherness was that quality which struck the father of the household all those years ago – that of religious or racial otherness.

In those terms, then, we and the baboons from *Wild Kingdom* have some common ground. If something is different to what we are used to, then more often than not it is regarded with fear and suspicion. For difference means change and dealing with change reminds us of many things. Mostly it reminds us that we are temporary, our lives are finite and so if together we can build community, and culture and a system of beliefs and values, then there is a sense of permanency given to us as a whole.

Otherness makes us question our certainty and consequently there is a fundamental apprehension, a fear about things and people that are different.

Sometimes the fear is passed down to children and sometimes the cycle is broken, because nobody is hard and fast in their character makeup. We are layered. And as such, even though otherness can be uncomfortable it can also enrich and add diversification.

There is a dividend paid when otherness is embraced, for it is a two-way interaction. It may take time but I think that is the key to living with the idea of otherness.

Why? Because of some fathers I knew.

Walking along Woody Point jetty I saw a wedding in the late afternoon, everything bathed in the lovely light that time of the day brings. Members of the wedding party clustered together on the grassed area at the beginning of the jetty.

I always like to have a bit of a look-see at a wedding; it's a couple's big day, a public display of commitment. And you don't get much more public than the Woody Point jetty.

There are picnic tables and playgrounds and a grand hotel that was once the humble Belvedere pub, of which my father would say, 'If you walk out with all your teeth intact in your mouth then that's a good night out at the Bell.'

I saw a man in a coloured vest and a tight-fitting suit fidgeting and talking a little too loud. This, I thought, was the groom.

Another man, in a grey suit, was prowling about by himself, with a folder in his hands. He looked a little like a detective about to go and give evidence in court, but I supposed he was the celebrant.

Another man, a little more steady but dressed the same as the man I took to be the groom, was standing alongside the fidgety man.

The best man?

No.

The two men held each other and then kissed gently on the lips.

Groom and groom, I supposed.

A photographer stood up from a crouch, camera in hand. 'Beautiful!' he cried.

I watched as hugs broke out between people. I recognised a bearded man as a kid I'd been at school with; he was, I remembered, one of the chosen manual arts students whose work had been held up as an example by the teachers as an 'Adequate Utensil'.

The fidgety groom cried out to him, 'Come on, Dad, come on,' and held out his arms.

The bearded man hugged his son and then his new son-in-law.

'So bloody good, so bloody proud,' said the bearded man. He was, I thought, close to tears.

'You're not going to go the sob, are you?' his wife sang out.

'Who cares if I do! It's a wedding, someone's got to cry,' said the bearded man.

I thought of how he must have felt to have his son marry the person he loved. To be able to be there and help celebrate his son's big day, for the community to recognise it and him to say to his boy how proud he felt. It almost made me forgive him that he was good at metalwork.

And I remembered how a few years earlier I walked along the beach in the town where I grew up. My name was called out and I turned to see the woman who had once been the girl I was friendly with. I walked over to the barbecue area where she stood with her family.

We chatted for a while and we laughed about the rissoles, gravy and savoury rice. The barbecue smelled of snags and onions mixed with rice paper rolls and coriander. She called out to her father to come and say hello. He was playing with his grandchildren. One had fallen and he picked her up and cuddled her and made her laugh with funny faces.

Another man of similar age stood close and waved at the little girl.

'She'll be right, two granddads to spoil her,' said the girl I had known.

Her father and the other granddad came over and said hello.

'Grandkids wearing you out?' I said.

'No way. Love 'em. They're just too much fun. This is the latest edition. My son's girl.' And he held up the small child.

His granddaughter smiled at her pop and pulled at his cap. Her other granddad waved a finger. He was Vietnamese, as was his wife and his daughter.

The two old men laughed together. The boy who had wanted to watch the baboons fight had grown up and married a girl with Vietnamese parents.

The very people this proud old grandad had raised his eyebrows at, the otherness of them.

Time goes by and things change, and we choose, I suppose, to try and resist the change or we can be like the old man embracing his grandchild, and the bearded man hugging his son and son-in-law on their wedding day, embracing it and growing.

4

OTHER PEOPLE'S FATHERS, PART 2

*Y*ou learn a little about yourself, both as a child and as a father, through other fathers.

It is true that a great part of the joy of being a father is simply hanging about with your kids, but both the father and his children must also live their own lives. This is where the idea of Dad Time becomes something separate to the children, and the personality, makeup and character of a father can be expressed.

A boy I knew at school had a father who seemed constantly on the verge of exploding. He was one of the most nervously intense and cantankerous grown-ups I ever met, more volatile even than Krakatoa, East or West of Java. His basic state of being was set at simmer, and it didn't take much to set him off.

He was volcanic even when indulging in his passion for gem-setting in a strange secretive little room he'd built beneath his back stairs. He was a member of one of the local lapidary clubs but needed, he said, his own space where he could get away from the chatter of his fellow members.

He would mutter about a run-in with a chatterbox at the club before disappearing into the prison-like room, not unlike the one occupied by Steve McQueen when he was sent into 'the cooler' in the movie *The Great Escape*. Only instead of tossing a baseball against the wall and catching it repeatedly while plotting another escape attempt, as our Steve did, this father would go about the fastidious business of gem-setting.

It must have felt like a sweatbox in Redcliffe's subtropical summer.

'No noise,' he would say. 'I want my quiet time to enjoy myself.'

We'd hear muffled frustrated groans when the precision of his Dad Time hobby got too much for him, and we'd quietly peek through a little window and see him, bent over a gem-setting plate, a creature bathed in a bright light.

The magnifiers on his eyes made him look like a strange insect or some deep-sea fish as he strained over his gems.

When he stuffed something up, he'd ball his fists then silently scream. A Munch gem-setting 'Scream'. Made you wonder how much enjoyment he derived from his leisure time away from his occupation as, of all things, a flight traffic controller.

Surely your leisure time should be a refuge from work?

When he would reappear from his incubator under the stairs, he would be drenched in sweat, head for the beer fridge and pour himself a shandy – two parts beer, two parts lemonade – and sit on a vinyl striped chair underneath an elkhorn plant and very intensely, very slowly, drink the shandy.

My family's male grown-up, my father, chose a more basic form of leisure which could sometimes be quite profound. The snooze. He had an ability to sleep anywhere when he wanted to get away from it all. It was nothing to come home and see him prone on the tray of one of his trucks or stretched out in state on a trestle table in the backyard, dressed in stubbies and striped t-shirt. You'd go about your business until he woke, clapped his hands and said 'Lovely.'

I asked him if he dreamed when he snoozed.

'If I do, it's my business.'

I asked my mother where he'd found the gift of dropping off whenever and wherever he wanted.

'Well, I suppose if you've fought in a war you find ways to sleep in almost any place.'

My father adored snoozing. 'A chance to start the day again and the only coot who never got any benefit from a nap was Hamlet – too much perchancing to dream. Stupid bugger.'

It seemed to me that Dad Time in its purest sense was something a father could immerse himself into and also share if he wanted to or was asked to. I once went on a hike with a schoolmate and his father because the father had been tasked by his wife to spend a bit of time with his son.

The father was a member of an orienteering society that would march out into scrubland and wander about for a weekend.

Mr Orienteer had little interest in his son coming – or me, for that matter.

'Bring a mate,' he'd told his son. 'Bring someone you can muck around with because I don't want you holding me up. Okay?'

When he picked me up, I sat in the back seat beside his son. Mr Orienteer turned his bearded head towards us.

'Now listen, I've made some special scroggin for you, okay? Don't touch it till we get there. It's special scroggin, just for you, okay? But keep your hands off your scroggin. Okay?'

I stared back and my chum didn't say anything. Mr Orienteer nodded and turned back to the wheel. 'Okay' was all we said.

As we drove, he would shoot looks at us in the rear-view mirror. I think he was checking to see if we would touch our scroggin. I had no idea what scroggin was, and my schoolmate didn't look that interested in anything really. It sent a bit of a chill through me because, even though I wasn't sure what Mr Orienteer was on about, I thought that scroggin might be a derivation of the dreaded 'scragging'.

This was the word given to the terrifying idea of a group of boys taking another and rubbing toothpaste on the wretched victim's penis. This, I learnt from another friend's elder brother, was what happened in the air cadets and he informed us that 'scragging' was all the go on the air cadets' weekend camp. Was Mr Orienteer threatening us with some form of weird bushwalking hazing? A special scroggin?

I asked my silent chum what scroggin was.

He shrugged his shoulders and pointed to a box on the floor.

Mr Orienteer flicked his eyes to us.

'You okay?'

I stared back.

'Okay?'

'What's scroggin?' I said in a tight voice.

'Scroggin? Scroggin is scroggin,' Mr Orienteer said as if he were talking to an idiot.

'What is it?' I asked again.

'Scroggin is . . .' Mr Orienteer was a bit perplexed. 'Can't believe you don't know what scroggin is. It's . . . nuts . . . and stuff.'

This didn't help me feel any more comfortable.

'Nuts and stuff. Energy food, for hiking. Snacks to keep you going.'

I stared.

My friend sighed and picked up a plastic container from the floor. He shook it.

'This stuff is scroggin,' and he began to take off the lid.

'Keep your hands off your scroggin!' snapped Mr Orienteer.

'I'm just showing him, Dad.'

'Okay, okay, but don't touch. Don't touch the scroggin. Okay?'

'I'm just showing him,' said his son.

There were three plastic pouches inside the container. One was filled with nuts and dried fruit and a few odd-looking food bars.

The others were filled with chewing gum and Mars Bars and packets of potato chips and some large bottles of Coke.

'That's your special scroggin! Okay?' said Mr Orienteer.

His son slowly put the lid back on and snapped it shut.

•

We drove past Caboolture, which in the 1970s seemed like the last outpost of civilisation in south-east Queensland, and after we left the concept of bitumen roads behind, Mr Orienteer would look at us in the back seat and repeatedly ask, 'Okay?'

My friend stared out the window.

We eventually parked in a paddock along with a series of other outdoor four-wheel drive cars and all the people who got out of those cars looked almost the same as Mr Orienteer.

A group of beards, funny little sunhats, knapsacks, long socks and shorts with lots of pockets proceeded to stagger about into a circle and whip out compasses and maps.

Even though the 1970s was a hair-grower's and stylist's delight, these beards weren't manscaped in any way; all were long and bushy, a bit like those on portraits of Australia's early European explorers, and they added to my feeling that these people were a definite group, a cult almost. So strong was the feeling that even the women who were amongst us gave off the impression of having beards.

It was quite unsettling. We didn't seem to belong, my school chum and I, and Mr Orienteer was quite aware of it.

'Okay. Now we've got our track figures worked out, and we don't want to be held up too much. Okay? We might get into it. Okay?'

We stared at him.

'Bit light on marshals so you might want to help here? Okay?' he said.

Mr Orienteer and his son stared at each other for a while and then the silence was broken with an 'Okay'.

I thought that 'we' meant the rest of the bearded gang, but the beard cult splintered into pairs and trios. My friend looked at his father and a woman who stood just behind, clipping down buttons on a pack.

'Okay?' said Mr Orienteer.

'Okay!' said the woman. And they marched off, striding away from us at a fair crack, never looking back.

I looked at my friend, 'What are we doing? Are we following them?'

He shook his head. We were staying here with a few other 'marshals', people who couldn't or wouldn't embark on the trek: an old woman and her son who wasn't quite right and sat playing with his snot, and another older man with a limp who set himself up under a tree and listened to the races.

I thought it odd that my schoolmate wasn't even allowed to have a go at participating with his father in a Dad Time activity and I felt a bit sorry for him.

'You okay?' I asked him.

He shrugged then said 'Okay!' like his father and laughed a little. 'I've seen what I had to. Let's get stuck into our scroggin.'

I didn't quite know what he meant at the time but it made sense later.

His mother had suggested that their son might like to share in Mr Orienteer's pastime of traipsing around the bush with his beard as a pretext for finding out who his orienteering partner was. She had her suspicions that Mr Orienteer might be traversing different non-topographical, and more biological, contours and she was right. He was having an affair with a work colleague who was also in the orienteering club and all those furtive looks in the rear-view mirror must have been Mr Orienteer trying to figure out what his son was up to, whether he could be simply bought off with a 'special scroggin' pack or if he was on an espionage mission for Mum.

It was all sort of pitiful.

A while later, as I was riding down to work at Coles as a shelf-stacker and bag-packer, I saw Mr Orienteer and the woman he went walking off into the bush with going into a coffee shop. His foot was in a cast, so I supposed there wouldn't be much action in the orienteering club and if he did venture out it would be as a 'marshal'. I wheeled around and, as I rode past again, he was attempting to wrangle his crutches and to sit down. Not being able to resist the temptation, I yelled out at the top of my lungs, 'Don't touch the scroggin! Okay!'

•

The perfect flipside of Mr Orienteer was Ray Frawley.

Ray Frawley was a mechanic, local politician, perpetual community volunteer and all-round good bloke. When he was on the local council, and later mayor, he would come from council meetings unable to relax or let go of all that had been talked about around the council chambers. He would disappear under the house till all hours in his dad cave, reboring motors and inventing gadgets of all types, even coming up with an illuminated civic sign that showed people where notable landmarks and essential services could be found. When he needed a hand, he would wake up one of his sons by banging on the floor of their bedroom and then dragging them down in their PJs and slippers to help weld, rivet or ratchet together whatever it was he had created in his dad cave below the family home.

My father always said talking to Ray when he was 'on' made you get a stitch because he was so full of ideas and was always in a hurry to try and 'get on the job and get things done'.

Ray was uniquely old school in a few ways and calling him a firm believer in direct action is an understatement. During one council meeting, which was dealing with the interminable delay of a tree being removed due to concerns of it being safe to do so, Ray abruptly left during the debate with a nod of his head and wag of a finger, saying cryptically, 'Got to get on.' He returned about an hour later, covered in sawdust and cobwebs, took his seat and ended the debate about the tree removal by saying, 'All done and dusted. Went home, got me chainsaw and cut the thing down and chipped the lot. Done. Got to get on.'

During his tenure as mayor he'd get the local police sergeant to check up the 'credentials and wherewithals', to use his own words, of any fellow who was going to take one of his daughters out on a date.

He went camping and hunting with his kids but he took things a step further and became, of all things, a renowned expert on the Colt 45 handgun quick-draw competition, competing under names like Duck Holiday or Quiet Earp.

All this from Woody Point.

Ray's funeral was one of those ceremonies when the shroud of a good life falls over everybody attending, when the goodwill shared overcomes the grief, and sails are filled with the breath of a fine life. His children all spoke with a warmth almost as if he were still with them, and, in a way, I suppose he was. Perhaps that is what can come from a father sharing his Dad Time with the people he most adored.

•

Sometimes Dad Time can reach the level of David Attenborough documentaries or legend – the pink flamingos of Camargue, the feeding congregation of the whale sharks at Isla Mujeres in Mexico, the gathering of the Jedi or a meeting of model train enthusiasts.

An event which is welcome to all and yet seems to be the domain of that mythic figure, the middle-aged man, near to retirement age. Wearing a cardigan, if it's a cold day.

All sorts of people love model trains but, as clichés go, there is something wonderful about men of a certain age with a utopian world of order and precision. And almost all seemed to be fathers.

My father-in-law adored trains of all shapes and sizes; he was a father who felt comfortable in a room full of other fathers and perhaps this was why he invited me, the husband of his middle daughter and the father of his youngest grandchild, to accompany him to a model train display of a huge scale.

'I don't know, William, it may not be your, your, you know, thing but I quite like it.'

And, in one way, what's not to like? If you had lived long enough in this world, as men like my father-in-law had, and seen and experienced how transport and social systems work, how slow public transport infrastructure seems to take to come to fruition – then why not build your own little immaculate worlds of rail?

The grass is neat. The sidings and signs all work. Motorists wait patiently at level crossings. There are no delays. No ticket system breaking down, no vandalised carriages. No queues, no groups of grumpy commuters feeling harder done by than they probably are, no fare evaders hiding from ticket inspectors and transit officers.

Everything is perfect.

And yet, in this Lilliputian collection, there is magic.

My father-in-law loved trains and he adored model trains. He was a civil engineer and was a part of that generation of Australians whose life's work was building a nation through providing great works of public infrastructure. Like the Snowy Mountains Scheme and the country's networks of railways, dams and roads.

Some people say the environmental effects are a dark side of nation-building, and they have a good point, but that period of post Second World War endeavour and challenge has the glow of achievement. A time fuelled by a sense of optimism and purpose we occasionally look back on with a sense of loss. It was the time when men like my father-in-law were young and building what they thought was a nation for tomorrow.

Australia seems to be a society that is always in a state of flux, something is always on the go, even if we have a tendency to sometimes stick our heads up our clackers and forget how blessed we are.

I think in the world of models, and precision and order, men like my father-in-law found a delightful hobby but also something to cling to, a certainty they may no longer feel.

The trains nearly always have a retro feel, like the trains and landscapes of their youth, a time perhaps when they had a future in front of them as young men, a time before wives and children even. A time when their life was their own.

I have a colleague who has a father who is a model train enthusiast. She has, it would be fair to say, a problematical relationship with her father, in her own words, on 'a minor, First World level type of thing'.

'Nobody abused anybody, nobody hurt anybody, we all see each other at Christmas and Easter and we always ring each other on New Year's Day. It's just that my dad disappears into his train world. Nicks off to his safety room when things get a bit much.'

Isn't that what hobbies or Dad Time is for, I say to her.

Her view is that her old man hides himself in this world of control and it's a part of him not wanting to accept change.

'He's a white, late middle-aged guy who can't cope with getting older and how things have changed since he was a young man.'

'Yeah?' I said.

'Yes. He's been listened to almost all his life and he can't quite understand how everyone should be listened to, and how he should listen. And when you ask him to listen he just heads off to train world. He's Gulliver and the Lilliputians don't talk back, just the way he likes it.'

She loves him, she says. 'Of course I do, but he drives me batshit crazy sometimes.'

I listened and a part of me thought, I wonder if my daughter will ever talk about me like this? And a part of my brain, some corner that hopefully will make itself heard, made a note to 'LISTEN'.

•

One morning, out of the blue, I received a text. It was from a mate of mine and something made him send a general text to his mates. 'Today is my 54th birthday. My father died of a heart attack when he was 54 . . . but somehow I can't resist eating a second bacon and egg roll for breakfast.'

He's a few years older than me. We met when we were students at drama school and I laughed reading the text in the same way I have laughed countless times at the words and stories that have come from his mouth since we met.

But the text wasn't just funny in a gallows humour way, it spoke to a deeper connection between fathers and sons.

The basic rule of thumb that in some way you measure your own life with those of your parents. Some people are like my mate on his birthday with that text, understanding the finite nature of life, that we all come and go. Other people take it way too far and engage in an intergenerational competition of achievement.

People like Lone Wolf McQuade.

I first came across Lone Wolf at drama school and my time there coincided with the beginning of the New Age ideas of health, movement and life. This was basically a boon for old hippies and odd bods who suddenly found some use for their dabbling in things such as massage, yoga and any variants of said 'disciplines'. The whole thing was a flipside to the increasing phenomenon of the Yuppies, an acronym now gathering dust but then on lots of lips. Young upwardly mobile professionals.

There were even some exponents of bridging the two streams of 1980s thought and where else but a drama school in Perth would you find them?

Lone Wolf wasn't a student or a teacher; instead he was an enthusiastic fellow traveller. He was in his late forties or early fifties and was a part-time lecturer in some humanities stream subject that was a part of the university to which the drama school was attached.

I first noticed him in the refectory. He was dressed in a hybrid style, if you were trying to be polite, and if you weren't you'd probably say it was a pure example of schizophrenic fashion. He was standing in line wearing tight blue jeans, black kung-fu slippers and a cheesecloth shirt without buttons that was fastened around the waist with a black tie. He had a fountain of ginger hair bunched together with a crimson bandana. He had a knapsack slung over his shoulder and was playing Neil Young's 'Old Man' on a purple ukulele. He also had a sculptured beard and mo, and this, added to the rest of the outfit, was enough for one of we drama students to say, 'Didn't know Chuck Norris could play the uke.'

This was topped by, 'Yeah, it's Lone Wolf McQuade, the musical.'

Lone Wolf McQuade was one of the more delightfully ridiculous cinematic offerings of the 1980s, a film thrown together with table scraps from the Dirty Harry franchise and Sergio Leone westerns with a bit of *Mad Max* thrown in as well. Although instead of Clint Eastwood we had a kung-fu ranga, Chuck Norris as a lone Texas ranger wearing a hat the size of the state of Texas.

He looked like a vigilante mushroom as he battled leering Mexican bandits and evil cigar-eating drug lords.

Nothing made sense and that was half the fun; he got buried in his turbo-charged runabout, and after being knocked unconscious, revived himself and freshened up by taking his shirt off and cracking a can of beer, which he then proceeded to pour over his body. He then turned the ignition on his subterranean jeep and flicked the turbo charge and the thing shot out from the ground like a submarine's trident missile breaking the surface of the sea.

It was operatically ludicrous in a mundane second-hand way, which sort of summed up ukulele Lone Wolf. He would come to shows we drama students put on, knew a lot of the musicians at the Con and was also a dance aficionado. He seemed to be across a lot of the new movement and meditation methods of the eighties and, Perth not being that big a town, we bumped into him quite a bit. He was a man who seemed to be constantly trying to find a new skill, a new trick, if you like, to apply to the whole process of living, and he would jump from new idea to new idea like they were a smorgasbord of theories. He was a heightened version of someone like Ray Frawley but, unlike Ray, his restlessness would get the better of him and he would leave things undone and half finished.

He would mix and match his practice of these disciplines with varying results, as illustrated when he said he was a student of kung-fu and ballet, the two being much closer than we might think. He invited us to visit his 'dojo' anytime, a dojo being a hall or room where a martial art is practised and refined. Only Lone Wolf's was part martial arts dojo, part homemade still for his brewing, part recording studio, part hydroponics lab, part home gym and part storage facility for his collection of junk. 'Life's crap' he called the pile of flotsam and jetsam that sat in one corner. He showed us how he would meditate to the unique accompaniment of old episodes of *Pot Black*, the British snooker show. He would sit cross-legged in front of his Rank Arena TV and watch this mad program of coloured balls being chipped around a billiard table by men with broken faces and sharp eyes, dressed formally in black with bow ties and vests. There was a strange introduction from a large bald man with big glasses who bellowed like he was trying to warn an oncoming train about a bridge collapse, while the commentator, Whispering Ted Lowe, whispered like an asylum inmate in some strange accent.

All the while another disembodied voice would yell scores, which were achieved by hitting the balls in the pocket, and a white gloved hand would remove the occasional balls from the hanging pocket and place them back on the table like a chef placing the last delicate morsel on a beautiful platter.

'It's the discipline and focus of the snooker players, the grand ritual of the game and broadcast that gets you. Takes you there. So powerful,' said Lone Wolf.

Where it took you nobody was quite certain, but Lone Wolf was sure he wanted to get there.

I stared in amazement as Lone Wolf put the show on and sat crossed-legged stroking his ginger chest hair. 'It helps if you're stoned, you know, lifts you to a higher plane.'

Hence the hydroponics lab.

He would demonstrate 'Fu Ballet' a dance method that he claimed combined the elegance of dance, the power of martial arts and the grace of both. It was basically like watching someone have a roaming fit of some sort, where he would kick and plié and squat and tap dance and bump and bang into things in his tightly packed multi-purpose dojo.

Gobsmackingly, all this was performed to the music of Winifred Atwell, a honky tonk pianist who supplied the theme to *Pot Black*, a repetitive jingling, tinkling tune which seemed to lift the movements of Lone Wolf's Fu Ballet to an idiotic art.

He was a funny, generous ratbag. Very hard to keep up with and, I suspect, be close to.

He was distanced from his family. His father, he said, had been a very successful real estate developer and was a corporate big man who never really tried to comprehend life or understand a meaning to existence other than to make money.

'You know, before I went to school some mornings, my father would sing out to me "Good luck". I'd say, "For what?" He'd say, "The race. Good luck in the race." I'd say, "What race?" and he'd say, "The human race." He'd always say, "Good luck in the race." As if everything was a competition, you had to achieve. Blindness, absolute blindness.'

Lone Wolf was also separated from his own children. 'They stayed with their mother, they had the whole middle-class house thing going on. Saturday sport, wearing the right type of blazer, blah blah blah. Cake-mix life.'

It seemed the more they achieved, the more willing Lone Wolf was to go in the other direction, to race at breakneck speed away from them. 'Just the way I am, just the way they are.'

The only time I met any of his children was one Saturday afternoon during a *Pot Black* pot meditation. A tall boy was leaving Lone Wolf's house and Lone Wolf introduced us: his teenage son had just popped in to say hello after a game of senior-school footy. We said hello while Lone Wolf went inside to fetch his car keys to drop his son back home.

'How'd you meet Dad?' the boy asked.

I told him through the drama school at uni. He nodded.

'He loves to put on a show,' the boy said quietly.

'Certainly does, a jack of all trades,' I said.

The boy nodded and laughed a little. 'A joke of all trades and master of none. That's what grandad said about him.'

'Well, he has a go,' I offered.

The boy nodded and smiled a little. 'Yeah,' he said softly.

And then we said goodbye.

It was odd hearing a son talk about his father like that, almost as if it was an effort to eulogise him, part fond remembrance and part forlorn lament.

And then I met Lone Wolf's father.

I was leaving classes for the day when I saw Lone Wolf and his purple ukulele in the carpark. He was heading to his car and he stopped when I said hello and asked what he was up to.

He looked at me and then said he was going to see his father. 'Would you like to come?'

I thought for a moment and then Lone Wolf simply said, 'Come.'

He looked, it struck me, a lot like his son at that moment.

I said, 'Sure,' and we drove across town to what,
I suppose, you would call a retirement home. It was quite
grand and well set up but smelt of chicken soup and the
passage of time.

We walked through a common room where a collection
of elderly residents sat, some seemingly mummified, their
heads tilted back and mouths open, some staring dumbly, all
barely moving. On the radio a song called 'You Make Me
Feel Like Dancing' by Leo Sayer played, a disco soundtrack
to a sedentary landscape in the common room.

We entered a room and there on the bed was an old
man, breathing the way that old men breathe in places like
that. When their breath is running out.

Lone Wolf stood looking at the old man, then pointed
at a seat for me. I sat and looked up at the man standing
there with a purple uke in his hands. He took a deep breath
and then said slowly, 'This is my father and he is dying.'

We sat listening to the old man breathe.

Lone Wolf put a chair by the bed and sat. 'I thought
about him. Thought about him this morning. How when
he'd say, "Good luck in the race." His joke, his dad joke.
His thing. But I'd forgotten how he'd say after that, "It's our
race, our only race." I'd forgotten that.' He let out a sigh.

'I thought he was just telling me life was a competition, but I thought this morning maybe he was just saying, actually, just saying good luck out there, stay safe and good luck. Be happy. Live well.'

He paused and then said softly, 'Fuck me.'

He picked up his ukulele, held it in two hands. His father, he said, loved a song called 'La Mer', a French song.

'He'd listen to it all the time, hum it. Bobby Darin did a cover of it in English but that was rubbish, he'd say, Darin's words were trite, meaningless.'

Lone Wolf said he had learned the song but had never really understood it. 'Thought about it today, it's a song about a bloke's life. Where he's lived, by the sea, how the sea has been a constant thing as he's lived. How it has sung a love song to him. Has rocked his heart for life.

'Now, Willy, that is a strange song for a corporate big guy to love. My father to love. My father,' and he paused before going on, 'is dying.'

And then, in that room filled with an old man's shallow breaths, he sang 'La Mer'. Slowly strumming on his ukulele, he sang it to his father.

I listened. It may have been played better, but never more beautifully. I listened. To a son saying to his father that he loved him.

•

Around a dinner table a group of us were talking about fathers. On what makes a father a father.

'Well,' said a teacher, 'it doesn't take much to be a father on one level, you just have to have a child with somebody, but I wonder if you can ever stop being a father?'

'What about sperm donors?' her husband asked.

'Do anonymous sperm donors ever think about their kids?'

I wondered if these donors thought in idle moments what their offspring might be up to and how they were faring in the world. Do they ever wake up one morning and wish them good luck in the race, the human race?

'Well, probably not, as the whole point of being an anonymous donor is to remain anonymous,' said the teacher.

'But if you are a donor,' a solicitor said, 'what rights do you have as a father if your donation becomes a living, breathing human?'

Talk turned to the American actor Jason Patric, who donated sperm to his ex-girlfriend Danielle Schreiber in 2009 so she could become pregnant. They had been in a relationship for several years and had actively tried to have a child. After their relationship was over and Schreiber continued with efforts to have a child, Patric donated his sperm, she became pregnant, had a baby boy and, after a time, Patric sought to have an active role in the boy's upbringing.

The issue has been in the Californian courts for some years with a series of rulings and appeals and counter-suits all trying to determine the status of Patric's fatherhood.

'Some fathers,' I said, 'take proprietary rights way too far.'

I was asked to fess up and elaborate. Was I talking about myself?

No, I said.

'Come on, tell,' the teacher's husband said.

I told them of the time I was going out with a girl who was very lovely and we had fun but the whole relationship was sort of finite because she was going to go overseas and I wasn't going to follow.

'A fling that gets serious,' said somebody around the table.

'Exactly, sort of, well, yes. I think,' I said, and not for the first time I was told that I was a boofhead and was ordered to get on with the story.

'Well, we began to get quite serious –'

'In a non-serious way,' interrupted the solicitor.

'Yes,' I said. 'And I was invited around to her parents' place for Sunday night dinners.'

'Here we go,' said another at our table and there were a few laughs.

I told them how after dinner was done, we'd help clean up and one night the father and I were alone in the kitchen. I was wiping a colander and he grabbed one side of it and pulled it towards him. The handle was quite small and I couldn't let go, so I was half dragged with it and then I understood that the father was doing it deliberately. He was pulling me close to him.

We were face to face, and he looked at me and said, 'I know what you're doing with my daughter. I know.'

I couldn't get my fingers out of the colander and had to stand there with this odd man muttering, 'I know what you do with my daughter.'

I managed to get my fingers free, took a step back and waved a tea towel back onto the rack.

'Well, I certainly hope not!'

It was an attempted joke but the father looked like he wanted to throttle me.

'With the colander?' said the teacher. 'Throttle you with a colander?'

'He was a very strange fellow,' I said.

'He's a father,' said the teacher.

'A strange father. When we all saw my girlfriend off at the airport she gave me a kiss and it was, well, you know, a farewell kiss so it was a bit of a show.'

'Describe *a show*,' said the teacher.

'Well, you know, a big pash, a real hamburger with the lot, and it went on for quite a time and when we finally finished her father just stared at me, as if we were still holding the colander and said, "She doesn't kiss me like that."'

One of the girl's sisters said, 'Well, Dad, she's not supposed to, she's your daughter.'

And we stood there with him giving me the colander death stare.

There were other tales of odd things fathers would say or do. The teacher remembered being at the fortieth wedding anniversary of her parents and the master of ceremonies asked her father what his best dad joke was.

'The old fart holds my hands and says in front of everybody, "My best joke is you." I mean, *me*, he picks out me in a family of six kids.'

The solicitor told how he was almost ready to commit his father after he repeatedly did 'tricks' with dentures. 'Crap like, taking his dentures and giving them to whoever had given him a present on Christmas morning and then holding them out in his hand and saying "Fang-you". Pathetic.'

There was another woman at the table, a dentist, who had been quiet for a bit and then said, 'It must be odd to some people, especially those men who want to have children and can't, or to a guy like Jason Patric who wants his fatherhood legally recognised – rightly or wrongly – that a man who has had children can simply opt out of being a father.'

There was a pause and then she went on.

This dentist's father had left her mother and her and her siblings years ago, when they were at a very early age. Over the years, he had stayed in some form of contact, occasionally taking them on holidays, turning up at weddings and twenty-first birthdays and then vanishing off back to his life. His 'other life' as they call it, for it wasn't a part of theirs.

The dentist said that she and her siblings would have loved to have a father who had annoyed, shouted at and cuddled them. Been cross or cranky, told them off and then maybe come back and half apologised for being mean. A father who mightn't have liked a particular girlfriend or boyfriend. Told bad jokes and forgot a birthday and then made it up the next day with an outrageous gift.

She wished that there had been a father to help their mother round out a family, even though she could not have wished for a better or more dedicated parent than her single mother. She would have liked something more than the man they occasionally see, always in a public place and at a time when it suits him, a vaguely familiar stranger who plays no real part in their life. And even though they chat about their children and their nieces and nephews with him, it's the way you would talk to an old neighbour or family acquaintance, and even that may be too generous.

'I'm sure fathers can be problematical but try not having one at all. Especially when it's by his choice. It's a bit of a different adventure.'

There was a look in her eyes, a quick sad look, that quickly disappeared but spoke of hurt and rejection and anger, made all the more acute because of its brevity.

'But,' she said, 'I suppose I can't really complain about something I never really had.' Then she laughed a little. 'Although I was shopping the other day and I overheard these two young girls, teenagers, who were trying to buy some pyjamas for their father's birthday and they were saying they couldn't find any bad enough for him. Is that a thing? A dad thing? Bad pyjamas.'

There was laughter, a chorus of 'Of course!' and the solicitor and I exchanged knowing looks.

Not that long ago, during breakfast at a café, the solicitor had said to me solemnly over a cup of hipster coffee that it was, as the song goes, 'Time to Say Goodbye'.

He told me it's always hard to say farewell to a close friend, and friends, he said, don't come much closer than a favourite pair of pyjamas. Or jammies, or jarmies or PJs or jim-jams.

I looked at him.

He held up a hand and said, 'These are non-human friends I'm talking about.'

I nodded.

'Call them what you want, William, there's more to pyjamas than you think and when the end has come one can't help but remember the things you've been through.'

I told my friend this talk was indecent, even in a hipster café, where some of the clientele seemed to be wearing variants of pyjamas as daywear. He called me out on this. I am a known recidivist PJs-in-public wearer.

I countered with the bold statement that the difference is I know I am wearing PJs out and about and not as selected fashion statements to advertise myself. This is an interesting pyjamas point because manufacturers of pyjamas these days seem to go in two directions: they make PJs as boring as possible so that they might go undetected as undercover sleepwear or so childishly stupid that you sport a fair chance of being arrested even if you go outside for a moment in the front yard at midnight.

My PJs are only displayed in brief excursions in the wider world – a panicked scuttling effort at putting out the bins when the rubbish trucks growl their way through the early morning street or a dash to the supermarket for milk or bread or some such needed household essential.

He pointed at me. 'I saw you in the bottle shop in your PJs!'

This was true, I admitted. 'Yes, household essentials.'

He stared at me and then shook his head.

'I don't care what you say, I am going to miss my PJs.'

There will be others, I assured him.

'No,' he said fiercely. 'Not like my sharkies.'

I put my cup down and asked him to explain himself.

His favourite pyjamas were covered, apparently, in sharks, or as he called them, 'Sharkies'.

I looked blankly at him. My mind went to the Cronulla Sharks, of which the term Sharkies is a common diminutive.

The idea of sleeping in garments festooned with images of Paul Gallen or Andrew Fifita is quite frankly something nobody should ever contemplate, but my friend explained that the sharks were a different collection of 'proper sharks'. After a pause, he added, as if I was an idiot, 'From the sea.' And pointed vaguely off to the left.

He then described the garments. 'Pure cotton, bought them in Spain at a market by the sea. On our honeymoon. My wife picked them. For me. Brilliant.'

He sighed. 'Hammerheads, grey nurses, tiger sharks, makos, thresher sharks and, yes, great whites. My kids went and found out all the types of sharks on my PJs.'

He must have had them for a long time.

'I used to keep them to wear on Father's Day. I used to think it was the kids who wanted me to wear them, but I think it was more me. Yes, Will, had them for years. Years.'

I nodded in understanding. I would have missed these PJs if they were mine.

How, I asked him, did he know that the time had come to say goodbye?

He nodded and looked off into the middle distance like some bad actor from a hospital soapie knowing the signs of a terminal prognosis. 'When the elastic went and the crotch gave out.'

He tried to clench his jaw and his voice almost broke. 'They weren't even decent if I was alone by myself in a dark room. Shame.'

'Time to say goodbye,' I said.

He nodded.

I remember how PJs used to be a sure way of telling the change in seasons. My father's short summer pyjamas – always with something printed on them like knights standing with raised swords, or stripes, or checks, or anchors – which would denote the more festive attitude to warmer nights of the year. While winter was nearly always down to business with one-colour flannel, perhaps with a band of different colour on a cuff or above a pocket.

'There's more to PJs than you think,' said my mate. 'I realised why I was so upset about them, about a pair of daggy PJs.'

'Why?' I asked.

'Because it's like I was losing those moments with my kids, my little girl counting the sharkies, a stupid dad thing to wear my special pants.'

'Jesus,' I laughed. 'They are just pyjamas.'

He nodded. He knew that, but it's also time passing, losing a little of yourself, just a silly way of understanding that we come and we go.

He laughed. 'I know, fucking stupid, pyjamas as a symbol of your mortality. Rarefied First World indulgent bullshit, but still, oh I don't know, I just love my kids.'

He shrugged and we both laughed.

'Sorry,' I said. 'Where is the connection here?'

'Pyjamas,' he said with a straight face, 'mean never having to say you're sorry.' He picked up his hipster coffee and, just before he drained it, he said, 'Thus ends the pyjamas homily.'

•

The pyjamas homily made me think of how sometimes a father's homily can make him a hero.

One of my oldest and closet friends was in Darwin to attend the wedding of one of his godchildren. He'd never been to Darwin before and so decided he'd see a bit of the place on a bicycle ride.

He wasn't far into his trip when he came across three figures: one with a phone, one looking at my friend and pointing to the third figure on the ground.

The fellow looking at my friend was a deckhand from the Philippines, out for a walk. His words were brief and urgent: 'No breathe, nothing.' The bloke with the mobile was fumbling with it, saying 'Calling triple zero.'

The figure on the ground was fit, lean, sports-attired; must have been on a morning run and fallen over.

My mate's first thoughts were, I'll just roll him over, tap his cheeks a couple of times, give him a shake and all good.

But . . . pupils fixed, dilated and skyward, mouth frothy, lips blue. No pulse.

He looked down at the prone figure. He'd done all he could and decided he had better just wait for the ambulance.

And then he looked again. This man, he thought, was somebody's son. Maybe somebody's father, somebody who loved this man would hear news about him that would break their hearts. Change their lives.

So, my friend performed CPR. Never having done this on a human being, he found what he thought was the general region and pressed.

No pulse.

Pinching the fallen man's nose, a breath straight into him and out came the sound of a person breathing their last.

A few more chest pumps. Nothing. Another breath, more volume this time. Straight in, straight out, same sound.

No pulse.

Not really knowing what else to do, my friend pinched the fallen man's nose even tighter and gave him a thorough shaft of air. He'd either burst his lungs and kill him or he was gone anyway. Then . . .

The fallen man's eyes fluttered. His mouth moved. He took an unsteady and none-too-confident breath by himself. His arm moved. He started blinking. He spoke. 'Where's my dog? Gotta find my dog.'

'He didn't have dog. He just fell,' said the Filipino deckhand.

The fallen man tried to stand.

'Just stay here for a bit,' said my friend. 'Just want to know you're okay before we look for your dog.'

The man tried to stand up.

He said he lived just up the road in a suburb which happened to be the other end of the country.

Disoriented.

The ambos and police arrived. The police took details, the ambos hooked up the fallen man, stabilised him. And my friend started crying. 'Bit shaken, don't do this too often,' he said to a copper.

'He's good now,' the constable said. She pointed at the man being loaded into the ambulance.

'Okay. I gave mouth-to-mouth. Should I get checked?' said my friend.

'For your own peace of mind, yes.'

'Thanks.'

Back home, my friend didn't tell his GP the whole saga, just the necessities. The doctor asked my friend if he'd given the man whose life he'd saved his name, so the man would know who to thank for saving him.

No, said my friend. The police had asked the same question. He'd thought and decided not to let the man know who had revived him.

'Why not?' I asked. What a mighty thing to have done, to save a man's life.

My friend's daughter draped an arm around his shoulder and said, 'Go on, Dad, tell William what you said.'

My old friend made what you would call a dad sound and waved his hand dismissively.

'Didn't say much.'

'Not much, no,' said his daughter. She laughed and poked her dad. 'Tell us what you said when they asked you why you didn't want the man to know who you were.'

My friend took a breath.

'Because maybe it was enough for that man to know somebody had revived him, and that somebody could be anybody. Of any faith, of any colour, man or woman. Be any fellow citizen of the world. And he should be grateful and believe in all of them.'

My friend's daughter spoke. 'My dad, this guy here, said, "It's important to believe in the decency of people."'

When my friend's doctor heard this, he was silent and then shook my friend's hand. 'Mate, you didn't just revive him. You resurrected him!'

I stared at my friend. He made another dad sound and his daughter kissed him gently on the top of his head and said softly, 'My dad,' and she walked off.

This father put a little bit of hope back out there in the world. For all of us.

Thus ends the father homily.

•

The things you think about while having a beer in the North Bondi RSL. The dreadlocked father was folding up his son's beach towel. 'You want to take the sea scallop with you?'

'Dad!' the little boy says.

His father laughs. The boy feels his board shorts. 'They're almost dry!'

'Yeah,' says his dad.

'I love 'em,' he says.

His dad smiles and they leave.

I drain the last of my frothy, stand up and look at the blue ocean beyond the beach. The sea. I think of Lone Wolf and his song to his father.

I take in the football still on the TV. The Storm have scored a try. It is being replayed in frame-by-frame slow motion.

I stand not far from the burly man, his daughter and the old man who is his father.

And like the slow-motion replay, the old man turns his head to the sea and says slowly, 'Sea. Our beach. Our beach.'

The burly man holds his hand. 'Oh Dad.'

And I turn from them and the view, from a room with other people's dads, and hum a tune as I leave. 'La Mer'.

5

THE THINGS YOU THINK ABOUT WHEN SHOPPING

*I*t was around my daughter's seventeenth birthday that I remembered the teacher from primary school, the one with the limp who I'd seen shopping at the supermarket. In those days, my tiny brain had wondered why a father would be out picking up the food for the week. It wasn't the way things were supposed to work.

Fathers didn't shop.

I remembered him when I was looking at breakfast cereals, wondering what healthy middle-aged, high-fibre miracle bran I could purchase but knowing there was a very good chance that I would leave it unopened in the pantry until it collected a little civilisation of weevils inside its packaged universe before being tossed into the bin.

What prompted the memory was me picking up a variety pack of breakfast cereal just before I moved on to the bran. A collection of individual, single-serve boxed cereals stuck together, ranging from the supposedly healthy like Sultana Bran to the more fun like Coco Pops, Rice Bubbles and Froot Loops. They were always bought as a treat, perhaps when a family was heading off on a camping holiday or as a birthday present to round things out. That's why I bought them for my daughter: a daggy bit of throwback fun from the days when she was a little girl, when seeing a set of boxed cereals, something special that she hardly ever had, would make her eyes grow as big as saucers. Probably not because the little boxes in themselves were worth the excitement, but the mere fact that they were given at all meant that something special was happening, a birthday.

It was my wife who started it, when my son was little, and then later both the kids would get a pack. 'Just a bit of daggy fun, sort of sweet that something so silly means so much,' she said.

I was still holding the variety pack in my hand while looking at the bran, when I thought of the teacher with a limp. Men do lots of things today that they didn't do, or appeared not to do, when I was a boy at primary school. That is because the world changes and we change with it; that's the way of life.

But it was my mother's words that I remembered now. When I had looked at the teacher with the limp, his shopping list and his awkward trolley careering in the aisles of the supermarket.

'That man's a widower,' she had said.

I had no idea of what that meant.

'His wife died, so he has to do the shopping for his family, all right? He's got a couple of little girls to look after as well as teaching the likes of you, so just watch yourself.'

A widower. His wife had died.

I dropped the variety pack into my shopping trolley.

I had had no idea that one day I would be like the teacher, a widower, but how would anybody know that could happen in a life? Especially as a child.

But that was what I had become, and that was why I found myself doing a lot of things as a father that my father hadn't done.

Like shopping; although, unlike the teacher with the limp, I never quite managed to take a shopping list with me. That would have been a bit too efficient.

I think my father missed out a bit with not doing the weekly shop because I had discovered that my own family shopping, which entails mooching around the aisles with my mob, can be quite fun.

When the kids were little we would drift around on a Thursday night doing the weekly shop, me, my wife, our son, our daughter, a little wagon rolling through the prairies of the market. Our son would perch on the front of the trolley and our daughter would sit in the little foldout seat at the back of the trolley, her legs poking through the mesh and then jiggling as we pushed along. The kids would point at stuff they knew they weren't going to get and laugh, try and work on their maths when asked questions by their mother.

We would wait a while at the delicatessen counter, while the staff members would slip some small treat to the little ones: an olive, a bit of ham or maybe some dolmades.

And even when things might have been a bit strained it was still time together as a family. Perhaps the crowds in the shops were too heavy or my wife and I were cranky with each other over something – something that relatively content couples get cranky over. Or maybe one of the kids was cracking the sads over something they had seen shopping, and they knew in their two-year-old's soul that they couldn't

157

exist without that small packet of sultanas. 'Tarnaaaaaaaas,' they howled with every breath they could muster.

Or perhaps just when you'd made it to the checkout, there'd be a Kinder Surprise or a Cadbury's Furry Friend chocolate that they wanted and weren't allowed to have and they'd explode howling.

Nobody else ever said anything, because we were just a family out doing the shopping, and on that particular day the kids might have been a bit scrappy. Almost everybody has a time like that because that is what it means to be a family.

And one day, because life can be like this, there is just the three of us, my kids and me. Thirty-eight years after seeing the limping teacher in the supermarket, you become a widower.

Life can be like this.

Not a family with a mum and a dad. Just a dad. If it were a television show then maybe it would be like the programs I had watched in the afternoons when I was a kid. Maybe I went home after seeing the limping teacher and tuned in to a show about a motherless family and some half-wild animal. Something like *Skippy*.

But no, no family living in a national park having cheesy adventures with a marsupial. Just me and my kids and two mad kelpies called Ray and Delilah who don't do anything Skippy-like. They don't drive a power boat or pick locks or thwart evil-doers. They dig holes, drop poo, come for a pat and a cuddle and are lovely beyond all description.

There is a tendency at times to become a sort of hybrid parent, attempting to be a bit of everything, even though there are family and friends that will help in ways that you might not be aware of at the time, and may never be aware of. And the fact that my children dealt with the loss of their mother in many ways on their own as well as a part of our family group is also part of their story.

But it's this hybrid thing that can lead to all sorts of adventures even on the most domestic of levels. I only had to look into the shopping trolley to see the collection of stain removers under the breakfast cereal variety pack.

I could tell something wasn't right with my shirt. Taking it off the line, I thought it didn't look quite the same as the last time I wore it. I held it up in front of me before I put it on, realised I wasn't wearing my glasses and so went inside, put on the specs and held the shirt up to the light.

It had been a blue linen shirt. Now it had spots on it and had a hint of the Jimmy Hendrix about it – the purple haze.

I thought about whether there was any way it could be rehabilitated then considered briefly that it didn't look that bad and could be worn. Then, after a few more moments of inspection, I knew the garment was a goner. It wasn't the same size. Another donation to the op-shop bin.

I guessed the culprit was my old nemesis – a pen left in a pocket.

Washing disasters, everyone has them. Although some of us have a back catalogue of cleaning clangers bigger than the Beatles' hits.

There has always been an element of misadventure with me and anything to do with the laundry, and this is an area where I have spent a lot more time than the preceding McInnes generation.

I could get my head around things like Rinso and Fab and Omo but Reckitt's Blue and starch had me thinking that the whole idea of the laundry was actually more like a mad scientist's lair.

Take washing machines. Growing up, there was a washing machine called the Pope which looked a little like a cross between a poker machine and the robot from *Lost in Space*.

Ours was given the nickname of Paul, who was reigning pope at the time.

There was a wringer on top of Paul's big drum through which you manually fed clothes. Invariably you'd get your hand caught in the wringer and then you'd have to smack a lever which would release it. My mother and father would yell 'Jackpot!' whenever the lever was pulled.

Just after my son was born I bought a dryer and washing machine from a fellow I met in a pub who said that they had fallen off the back of a truck. I asked him what he meant. He said they had literally fallen off a truck after an accident on the Western Highway. 'A bit of a ding here and there, but as good as new and cheap as chips.'

This pair of household appliances seemed a product of the American horror writer Stephen King's imagination, the washing machine possessed with a soul of evil. Glowering in a corner, it would make the oddest sounds and devour clothing.

The dryer was like some collection of howling souls, moaning like a grief-stricken cyclone.

And one Whirlpool we had was like a bucking rodeo horse you'd have to sit on to keep it from taking off on the spin cycle. I would perch up on top occasionally, holding my toddler son, and he would hiccup because he was laughing so much riding the Whirlpool bronco.

Apart from machines, there have been more mundane washing mishaps. Objects in pockets that should never see the inside of washing machines – pens, tissues, wallets, legal contracts and the cycle from hell when I put my phone, my daughter's phone and a pair of my glasses through the wash.

I gained a certain notoriety in the eyes of my children for once insisting that we could use dishwasher cube powder when we had run out of laundry powder. 'You've got to think outside the box, this stuff will work in a washing machine, but never put washing liquid in a dishwasher.'

'Why?' my son asked.

'It's like a special effects machine. Bubbles everywhere.'

'Really?' asked my daughter.

'Wise in the ways of suds am I,' I said in my best Master Yoda manner.

Of course, after this piece of advice, one rainy weekend we decided to put some laundry washing liquid in the dishwasher and watch the bubbles – only on the condition that I could play a compilation album from my vinyl collection. I figured that the dishwasher would be like the old effects machines that were on TV shows like *Countdown* and so it would be appropriate to have a *Countdown* era artist providing a tune.

We plonked on a record which featured rafts of different performers: '21 hits, 21 original artists' as the advertisements used to spruik or as I told my children, 'All the hits and none of the shit.' For some reason known only to the heavens, the dishwater put on an extra special set of bubbles to Murray Head's 'One Night in Bangkok' from *1985 Comes Alive*.

It became known as the bubble song.

It's not all Yoda moments though. After being a bit recreationally enhanced after a convivial and lengthy barbecue, I decided to do a load of washing and never lived down putting the washing through with methylated spirits as fabric softener. 'The bottles sort of looked the same. Sort of,' I lamely offered.

Even professionals have had their work go pear-shaped when I become involved. I had a suit and some shirts laundered when we were on holiday in Hong Kong. I rang up the services department in the hotel to give them my clothing and told the kids that at least no harm would come to the clothes because professionals would be at work.

They returned as a pair of tight leather pants with a snakeskin stripe and a red corset. I called the hotel desk, who assured me that their services department never made errors.

I asked a concierge to come and retrieve my laundry and when he saw me holding the clothing he gave me a deadpan look. 'You are either sadly deluded or unlucky in the matters of laundry, sir.'

When my clothes were returned, the concierge said, 'More appropriate, sir, but a little less interesting.'

I made sure I gave him a healthy tip.

I'm more than willing to put my hand up as a haphazard captain of the washing machine and, even though they may have changed from the days of my childhood and Paul, things can still go off track.

Even though I am still a work in progress, I like the idea that I am nevertheless the go-to person for advice in the minds of my children.

My daughter rang me about what to wash some of her jumpers in and, after I laughed and asked if she was sure she wanted the advice of a man who could be best described as a serial recidivist in jumper-washing crimes, she said, 'Why not, Dad, you seem to do a lot of washing.'

I laughed, there was a pause and then she said, 'Just tell me what you did and I'll do the opposite.' Sadly, she said it worked.

The other thing about our shopping trips was that, even when the kids got older, we would still go out as a trio to shop, walking slowly along beside the trolley, mooching about, picking things off the shelves and chatting. It was a way of being together in our family of three; a way of being together and sharing ourselves.

The local supermarket has a selected playlist continuously playing, supposedly to set a mood for shoppers to enjoy the whole consumerist experience. Or, as an old man from the assisted accommodation units who sits on the benches by the carpet cleaners wheezes, 'This music is brainwashing you. Brainwashing. Mind control.'

He was there tonight as we walked in and he said hello to my son, who had worked in the shop in his mid high-school years. My son stayed behind a bit and chatted to him, asked him how things were with him.

'I've got new shoes! New shoes. I've got new shoes,' he repeated.

'That's a good thing to have,' my son said.

The old man said, 'Mind the music.'

My son laughed a little. Pat Benatar's 'Hit Me With Your Best Shot' was playing. 'Righto, I'll try and resist Pat's subliminal message.' And he waved the old fellow goodbye.

My daughter said it was good how her brother had stopped to have a word.

'He does that quite a bit,' she said.

'Does he?' I asked.

'Yeah, he might smell a bit but he's got a good heart.'

I felt a bit proud and smiled and then pushed the trolley into a shelf and swore.

'That's karma for thinking it's all because of you,' laughed my daughter.

And a bit later the piped music began to play. It sounded familiar. I realised that I was going down the international foods aisle doing the 'Safety Dance'.

Men Without Hats. Was 1983 really that long ago? And why in hell can I remember the dance and the song and the bloody silly bunch of Canadians who made up the band?

Why? Because I'm an old coot. And it was such a stupid dance, perfect after a few too many recreationals at a party or at the bar of the students' club, because there weren't any steps involved, just some silly arm movements somebody came up with. Perhaps the old bloke on the benches had a point; the power of suggestion of the music played by the supermarket can lead to a middle-aged man time-travelling back to 1983.

'I think this band was a bunch of Canadians trying to be funny. There's a dance that goes with this, you know,' I tell the kids as we leave the international foods aisle behind us and walk down the next stacked alley of consumables.

'Sure,' they say, not really interested.

And so, by the tinned vegetables and canned fish, I do three or four intricate steps from the band's video clip, the odd arm movements in half circles with one hand stopping above your head, the other below your waist, and then reverse it. I half giggle and wince, wondering whether I have burst anything internally as I reboot the Men Without Hats no-feet-involved jig into the twenty-first century.

Then my kids do it.

'Not bad,' I say.

And for a while, in our home, if somebody wanted to go shopping or we were out of some basic foodstuff, the 'Safety Dance' move would be used as a form of semaphore signal that a purchase needed to be made. 'We're out of milk', for example, would be accompanied by one hand raised above the head, one below the waist and then reverse the order, and somebody would head for the milk.

When you are off shopping in father mode it can get a bit confronting. My daughter asked me a question one day that most parents get asked at one time or another. 'Dad, what is it that you do?'

The problem was the tone. It was a puzzled, almost embarrassed sort of tone that she shrouded her question in.

'Oh,' I said, 'a bit of this and a bit of that.'

She stared at me and I said, 'What did you mean?'

'What is it that you do?'

I looked at her, she looked back.

'What do you do to earn money?'

'Well, sometimes I act and sometimes I write, sometimes I go sit on a few boards here and there and sometimes I do a bit of this and that.' I smiled. And nodded my head. And said that the nice tuna in proper olive oil was on special so we should get a couple of extra tins. I thought I should add a bit of fatherly wisdom. 'Always buy canned tuna with olive oil, much better than the other stuff.'

She stared at me. And it wasn't that comfortable.

'You get paid for doing this and that?'

'Is that a problem?' I asked her.

'Do you know that Liza's uncle invented the twist and release Berocca drink?'

'Go away.'

'Well, that's what she said.'

'Well, good on him.' I was impressed.

So was my daughter.

'If he invented that twist thing, that is big-time this and that-ing. To come up with something like that.'

I couldn't argue. I knew I wouldn't be able to come up with the Berocca twist thing, I bet Liza's uncle was another one of those men who would have been good at manual fucking arts.

I was going to answer my daughter, and then I pulled at my belt. 'I act and I write, you know.'

I pulled at my belt again.

My kids watched me.

That morning I had added another eye to my belt with a corkscrew when my son asked me if I'd done my nude scenes yet.

'No, not yet.'

I was making a telemovie with a scene involving me romping in make-believe passion with another actor.

'Your nude scenes,' my daughter said.

Another shopper turned to look at me.

I said hello.

'Nude scenes, you?' said the woman, who lives in the next street along.

I pulled at my belt again.

'Thought you'd put all that behind you,' and she laughed.

My kids laughed.

I tried to laugh.

'Well, you know,' I said and I picked up some canned tuna. 'Cheap this week!' I added.

'Your nude scenes, that's how you earn your money?' asked my daughter.

The woman from the next street said, 'You'll all be having bread and dripping if that's how you earn what you eat!'

And she walked away, laughing.

I smiled and nodded and pulled at my belt.

My son and my daughter looked at me fiddling with my belt again and my son asked, 'You letting out or letting in?'

I told him I was letting out.

'Ah, moving into character parts,' he said.

I gave him a little bit of advice about what to do with himself.

'How long you got?' asked my daughter. 'Before your nude scenes?'

'A couple of weeks.'

'Good luck,' said my daughter, using the tone of a character from some bad war film farewelling a man on a suicide mission.

'I'll be right,' I assured them, sounding very much like the guy going on the suicide mission.

'Wooh, talk it up, Big Will! I've seen you at the beach, Dad – you've got a very good-paddock look.'

I admit this is true. I said as much to the movie's director and he assured me all would be fine. 'We'll fix it up with angles.' He nodded sagely.

I'd laughed. 'What does that mean?'

After another moment, the director smiled kindly and said he didn't know but it usually made actors feel better about themselves.

I tell my son this and he wants to know if I believed the director.

'Hardly, that's just the sort of things people say to shut up actors.' I go through some favourites for my children. 'That hair dye really matches your face', 'the bigger clothing size really makes you look slimmer', 'the performance can be saved in the edit room' and 'nobody will ever see it anyway'.

Ultimately, the poor sod of an actor sees themselves with a head of Grecian 2000 atop a middle-aged prune-face wearing a Demis Roussos–sized Bedouin tent and acting like a plank. Still nobody ever really sees it. Mostly.

That's the only near truth and the most unsatisfying element of the soothing treatment, because that's all actors want – their work to be seen.

Even my son is now vaguely interested as my daughter looks at me and asks, 'How do you do it, then?'

They both want to know how I'm going to go about it.

Well, I tell my kids, there'll be a few moments of unease and embarrassment but that's just par for the course. The basic formula is that you stare into each other's eyes, the woman usually opens her eyes quite wide and opens her mouth slightly and in the time-honoured tradition the man will intently stare with a sure gaze, clench his jaw in the age-old sign of deep passion and then you will press lips into the other actor's lips and almost invariably close your eyes and do your best to melt into each other.

'That's it? Is that a nude scene?' asked my daughter, inspecting a tuna bean mix meal in a tin before replacing it on the shelf.

'These things always look good on the shelf for a lunch, but I don't know.' She turned back to me. 'Isn't the whole idea of a nude scene to be, well, nude?'

'Yes, well, that's the theory.'

Some directors have been known to offer helpful advice to a pair of actors engaged in a love scene: 'Oil 'em up and we'll just roll camera and they can get on with it.'

Then you find yourself being slathered in baby oil along with your screen partner and you're both required to bounce and slither around each other like two vegies in a stir-fry.

Unfortunately, during these types of moments, actors usually try to demonstrate and give a little bit more and the sounds emitted from them are like those from someone enjoying a good meal. Lots of humming and half moans and the smacking of lips.

Nobody enjoys pretending to be in passionate love with a near stranger but occasionally it's the nature of one of the ways in which I earn my income.

'One of the ways?' asks my daughter, deciding on a rice and bean mix for school lunch the next day.

I nod.

One of the ways, because these days I suppose I have become a fully fledged slash person.

'Slash person?' asks my son.

If anybody used to recognise me it was usually as an actor. Or someone who might owe them money. But with more recognition you gain a slash. There are some slashes you don't want, Actor/Drunk or Actor/Tool, but Actor/Author is one that I will happily accept. Especially when I know I'm not the world's best actor or the world's greatest writer. It's something that is earned and in no way expected. You certainly don't want a three-way slash happening: Actor/Author/Tool.

'Yeah,' said my son. 'I get it, you don't want to be Ham Actor/podgy/sedentary/Hack author. Do you?'

'Oh Dad,' says my daughter.

'It's just a matter of sucking in the gut, closing your eyes and having a crack.'

My son shakes his head. 'Wow, you really are a thinking actor, Dad.'

'Well, we all have our method,' I tell him.

Strangely enough, a part of that method is simply accepting yourself for what you are. Or trying as best you can to do that, for perhaps none of us ever really accept what it is we are and what we look like. You only have to look at the number of weight-loss programs or appearance enhancers that pollute the world's airwaves, pages and websites. Promises of looking better than you are, of pulling the wool over the eyes of Mr Reality.

Well, there's not much point to that. I don't want to wear a 'William Shatner' – an actor's term for a constricting girdle worn under a costume to smooth the lines – or partake of the Israeli Army Diet or some equally freak-show weight-shedding initiative.

'I'll be right.'

I fiddle with my belt and think, I may have to go to work on the belt with the corkscrew again.

Panic.

'Holy William Shatner!' I say.

My daughter laughs a bit and then says, 'Wouldn't it be easier to invent the twist thing?'

And she throws a Berocca drink into the trolley.

•

Being a father out shopping can lead to a more perilous realisation, about how the society we live in sees your child.

It's easy to be a snob, but it's so utterly human to want to impress and pretend. I looked at my daughter and her friend. Both gorgeous young people. When I was their age, girls would slather themselves in tanning oil and fry their skin like dim sims in the sun, just because it looked good. Now, on this noisy Saturday surrounded by concocted advertising images of what the market claims are physical perfection, I think of how these two girls will have to navigate the minefield of fashion and fad, the pressure to look good.

And I know that a father can be a part of that problem. On another shopping trip, at one of those giant factory outlet sheds filled with brand names, we drifted through the tide of humanity trying to find some bathers for my daughter.

If any father ever thinks it's agonising waiting for a daughter to choose an article of clothing they should zip their lips, take it on the chin and wait for as long as they must, simply because it can be so hard for a teenage girl to know what to wear.

175

Pulling bits and pieces off the racks and then putting them back, second-guessing herself, looking over at me, it wasn't until an hour in that I had the sense to go and ask if my hovering around was putting her off.

'I mean, I know bathers are bathers. You can choose whatever you want and I'll just wait outside and you get, you know, what you want. I know bathers.'

My daughter looked at me and, after a little while, said okay.

I told her to text me when she was ready to buy something.

My daughter said okay.

I went and sat down outside. I thought I had gained some sort of sensible father achievement, a sensitive patriarchal level on a weekend shopping trip. And I waited. And waited. And the text came in: she was ready.

I went back into the shop, smiled and got my wallet out. 'My shout,' I said.

She looked at me.

'How'd you go?' I asked.

'Do you have to see it?' she asked.

'Okay, come on.'

She stared a little.

I told her it would be okay.

She didn't look sure, and to be fair, this was because I had a bit of form in this area. Once, when going on a socks and jocks safari for myself and my son, I decided to grab something for my daughter. I saw a specials rack in the women's section and recognised a brand that I knew my daughter had bought a few times. This was the go. The sizes would be on the hangers.

The more I looked amongst the items of underwear the more I realised that men's sizes were a lot easier to guess than women's because women tended to be a bit more specific. No 'M' for medium, 'L' for large or 'XL' for extra large that adorned men's fashion. The women's sizes seemed to be configured in some sort of layered mathematical formula and I thought about giving the whole thing a miss and heading off. I took a few steps away but then thought it didn't seem fair that my daughter would miss out. So I walked back to have a crack at picking something that might fit.

In a large mirror on a nearby pillar in the store, I caught sight of what I recognised after a few moments of consideration was a reflection of myself. A large barrel of a man in a billowing linen shirt, white shorts, Crocs, glasses and, on my head, my special fishing cap – a baseball-type cap with a very elongated brim.

It was designed for the man with a large nose, the brim pouring down over the front of your face creating a beak-like effect.

The reflection looked like a great swollen, bespectacled waterbird, wading aimlessly about in an undergrowth of women's undergarments.

I turned away from the mirror and back to the racks, thinking about how I must look. A middle-aged man faffing about, leaving, returning, then standing in front of a rack of bras and things – it isn't a comfortable picture, especially when some of the things probably weren't what a father should buy for his daughter just so she didn't miss out.

The brands on the coathangers didn't necessarily correlate to the garments that hung on them. This, I knew, was part of the DFO roulette, but the difference was a bit stark.

I peered at what was supposed to be a sports bra, ideal for my daughter's chosen sport of lacrosse, but the garment that was hanging on it looked like it was about as capable of offering any meaningful support as a cross-eyed gorilla was of solving a Rubik's cube.

I grimaced in annoyance and frustration and muttered as I tried to find a sports bra. 'This thing, this thing's no good. Well, I don't know.'

I heard a voice. 'Can I help you, sir?'

And I turned to see a staff member standing before me.

I repeated, 'Well, I don't know,' like a sad echo and stared at her.

She was about my age and had a smile on her face but also an incredibly intense deep-set glare, very nearly but not quite cross-eyed. If we were talking Disney animation, she'd be a very efficient mongoose.

'What can I help you with, sir?'

I am not sure if a mongoose would stalk a swollen waterbird but I certainly felt I was being appraised by some sort of carnivorous creature as I said, 'Well, this.'

'Sir?'

I grabbed the bra I had thought was a sports bra. 'This,' I said, and I proffered it to her. 'This hanger says a sports bra but this . . . garment thing isn't. Is it? Looks all meshy, you could sift icing sugar through it.'

She looked at the bra and then back at me with a quick eye-flick, like she didn't want me to get away.

'Sir, that is because it is an item of intimate apparel, not underwear.'

I looked back. 'Sorry?'

'Intimate apparel, not underwear. Although a sports bra is a specialised form of underwear it is still underwear, a functioning, purpose-built undergarment. This,' she deftly took the icing-sugar sift thing from my hand and continued, 'is an article of intimate apparel. Lingerie. Designed for aesthetic adornment.'

The great swollen waterbird tried to explain, 'Yeah, but . . . the hanger . . .' but ran out of puff.

The staff member gave me a quicker little flick of her eyes.

'Sir, what is it you are after and for whom?'

I took a breath and tried to explain. 'My daughter. I thought I would just pick up something for her and I saw on the hanger that it was a sports bra but then I couldn't see any.' I tried not to sound like an idiot and I pointed to the intimate apparel icing-sugar sifter in her hand.

'I mean . . . I know underwear . . . and I do know what lingerie is.'

Above the staff member's head, I saw the reflection again. I was pointing. And sounding a bit pompous. A common enough occurrence for middle-aged men, but that beaky cap took the whole thing to a new level of idiocy. Sure, a bloke who wore a hat like this would 'know what lingerie is'.

The staff member looked at me. 'Yes, sir.' She paused. 'Of course you do.'

I felt I had to explain and said simply, 'This is my special fishing cap.'

I stopped, knowing this wasn't going seamlessly.

'Yes, sir,' said the staff member. She almost smiled as she went on. 'The hangers can be a bit of a trap, the specialist underwear is over here, do you need a hand at all? Or do you know what you're after?'

Like an idiot, I held up a hand and assured her that no, I'd be fine.

I went to where she directed, grabbed a few things and left. I'm pretty sure I heard stifled laughter as I stalked off.

Later at home, I distributed the day's hunt amongst my tribe. Socks and jocks for my son, 'Good on you,' he said, and to my daughter her sports bras. 'Oh, thanks, Dad,' she said rather sweetly.

A few moments later, while I stood in the kitchen leaning on the big bench, she came prowling out and threw the bras at me.

'Why?' she said.

The bras landed on the bench in front of me.

'Why what?' I asked.

'Did you even look?'

'Of course I did.'

'Pick them up, Dad.'

I picked them up. I looked at them. I looked back at my daughter. I looked back at them. They were maternity bras.

Fucking hangers, I thought.

'Well?' my daughter said.

'I know underwear,' is what I said.

•

So that was why my daughter hesitated as I stood in the DFO swimwear shop asking to see what she had chosen.

'Look, you don't have to show me, I won't say anything, it'd be nice to see, that's all,' I said, trying to be an appealing, pleasant father. Or maybe that sounded a bit seedy so I said again, rather too quickly, 'No, no, no, that's all right, you're fine.'

There had been the odd occasion when I had foghorned quite loudly at the beach about some of the fashions on the sands. Why would you wear that? Why would you let your daughter wear that? My daughter had been quiet and maybe blushed.

Another father at my daughter's school had said how he and his daughter had had a massive row about what she had chosen to wear at the beach.

She had left the house in the morning in one outfit and then changed into another when she hit the sands.

The father found this out when he went for a run along the beach and came across her wearing 'some slip of a thing' washing the sea salt away at a beach shower. He had stopped and, in his words, had it out with her in front of her friends.

I winced.

'It's not like it's the 1960s, Will,' the man had told me. 'But I was really shocked.'

It all seemed a bit much to me, especially when the father had told me that he was jogging in only a pair of budgie-smugglers and runners.

He looked sheepish when he told me. 'I know, what a clown, but you know. She's my daughter.'

It's a bizarre get-out-of-jail clause that fathers seem to think they can use to explain or excuse going on an epic rant or when they behave like some belligerent cop from a bad movie, interrogating their daughters, their daughters' friends and making a bit of a scene. Standing in all their middle-aged glory encased only in a pair of budgie-smugglers. And runners. With socks poking out that have 'Bali' written across the top.

And so, in the shop, I told myself to shut up. None of your business. Let it be. Teenage body image, fashion trends. Not wanting to stand out but wanting to fit in, but nice to be noticed. It's a minefield for boys, maybe even worse for girls.

I nodded. And tried to smile.

'You don't have to, that's okay.'

My daughter shrugged her shoulders. 'It's okay. I've got a few things.'

'That's good,' I said.

'Here, what do you think?'

She held up something that looked like a combination of a red ockie strap and a small piece of luggage tied down.

I stared. I looked to the person behind the counter. She smiled approvingly.

'Very popular this year,' she said. 'A teeny-weeny micro one-piece teddy.'

'What is?' I asked.

'These bathers,' said my daughter.

I just continued to stare.

The teeny-weeny micro was passed to me. I looked at it. There was a tag, which seemed bigger than the garment, that said it was indeed a 'teeny-weeny micro one-piece teddy.'

'Bathers,' I repeated.

'Yes,' said my daughter. She looked at me.

I slowly shook my head and then tried to stop.

'Show him the others,' said the woman behind the counter.

My daughter produced a couple of triangles of green fabric and then something that looked like a slingshot. Even that would be too generous.

She looked at me. 'Well?' she asked.

I stood there.

'Christ alive,' I heard myself say. 'Christ alive, you can't, can you? Where do you wear . . . Christ alive.'

I stared at my daughter and then at the woman behind the counter.

They stared back at me and then exploded laughing. Gut-busting peals of laughter. A couple of other shoppers joined in.

My daughter held up a one-piece and a sort of retro bikini.

'These are what I got.'

I'd been had. Royally.

She looked at me and said, 'I know swimwear!' and laughed again.

The woman behind the counter wiped her eyes as she put the teeny-weeny micro thing and the slingshot away in a sorting box and then we paid for the swimmers my daughter had chosen. I waited till she settled down and I asked if people actually wore those other things. She said,

'Who knows, but good luck to them. Your face.' And she laughed again.

•

Clothing adventures tend to crop up when your children get on a bit and seem to stay at home longer than previous generations.

My son told me quite breezily that thirty is the new eighteen.

'What do you mean?' I asked

It meant he was hanging around home until he finished university.

'Till you're thirty?' I shrieked.

'Well, you've got to have a safety buffer,' he said.

'Good luck with that.'

The problem with having one of your offspring living with you who is roughly the same size is that articles of clothing can get mixed up.

I once picked up what I thought were my dark blue pants from the laundry and pulled them on with a bit of a struggle, thinking to myself that I really should do something about my good-paddock excesses if my chinos felt tight around my calves as well as my thighs. Nevertheless, I got them on and got to my meeting.

As I walked into the room, there were a few stares and then a producer friend asked with a deadpan face, 'Are we wearing our mid-life crisis, Will?'

I stopped, looked down and realised I was wearing my son's skinny-legged drop-crotch jeans.

'I've got my boy's jeans on.'

'William!' said the producer. 'We have had a sea change, haven't we?'

There were a few titters and I tried to clarify why I was wearing what I was wearing. 'My son's strides, I'm wearing my son's pants. By mistake.'

Not long after my tutorial in intimate apparel and undies from the mongoose at the DFO, I came up with a plan to mark a demarcation line in the use of underwear in our home. My large son was not averse to occasionally taking a pair of functional undergarments off the line without caring who the owner might be. Just as long as they were clean. While his preference for hygiene was admirable, his lack of appreciation in regards to proprietorship was not. It was a bit too commune-like for myself and, after doing my blob at him, I came up with a system that I believed would alleviate functional undies transgressions. I would buy a particular brand and he would buy another and, to ensure that the system was foolproof, it would be colour-coded. I would have plain and he would have patterned. Simple.

Until one morning when he was heading out to uni and I was trying to get ready for a photographer who was coming around to take some head shots.

I had been out dusting up the treadmill in the shed and was racing from the shower when the front doorbell went. The dogs barked, I yelled and hobbled as fast as I could to get changed.

'Hey, open the door and let the photographer through to the sunroom, please, I'll just zip into my room and get changed.'

'Righto,' my large son with a good heart said as he was pulling a polo shirt over his head.

'Than–' and before I could finish saying thank you, I saw above his jeans a hint of functional undergarment that wasn't patterned.

In fact, I could tell it was a pair of my organic bamboo functional undies.

The polo came down just as he opened the door and said hello in his friendly way and let the snapper in right at the moment I went off.

'You're wearing my bamboo undies!'

He turned as the photographer stuttered into the hallway.

'Pardon?' said my large son.

'My bamboo undies! There's no pattern. Yours are the patterned ones. You paid no attention to the system.' I couldn't help myself, my son's insouciance turned me into a ranting lunatic. A ranting lunatic covered in only a towel.

I sounded like an admonishing talkback host and quickly reached an infuriated Alan Jones level, as if I were dressing down a politician who had displeased me and my listeners.

I couldn't stop. I went beyond Alan Jones and got caught on a screaming jag. 'Simply not good enough, NOT GOOD ENOUGH!'

I heard myself sounding like a mad housemaster. Organic bamboo functional undergarments can do that to you, but I managed to offer the photographer a brief apology and told her to make herself comfortable in the sunroom while, scowling at my son who smiled pleasantly, I disappeared into my room and threw on some clothes.

I emerged a bit later, smiling and hopefully calm, and asked the photographer if she wanted any tea or coffee.

She smiled a little awkwardly and said that she was fine.

I thought I owed her another apology and explained how silly it was but I couldn't stand how he, meaning my son, wore my things. And I laughed again. 'My bamboo undies!' Just to underline what a ponce I was.

The photographer looked at me as I did up a stray button on my shirt and she said in an understanding tone, 'Don't apologise, please.' She nodded her head sympathetically so I nodded mine. She sighed. 'It's just so awful when your partner takes you and your things for granted.'

I went very still very quickly, which I think concerned her.

I stared at her. Two fellows, one putting on a shirt as he opens the door, the other one in a flap with a towel around him – this photo snapper must have thought, 'Okay, lots of art on the walls, eclectic-type house, writer/actor/ bohemian/arty/person. Seen it all before.'

Well, she well and truly had the wrong slash person.

This time I didn't go Alan Jones or demented house-master, I went straight to a Saturn V rocket with a bit of Mussolini thrown in.

The sound I emitted made the dogs run out the dog door, jump off the verandah and disappear under the passionfruit vines.

I thought I could see the fruit shake.

I started explaining, with a few adjectives thrown in, that my 'partner' was in fact my son and I went over the whole breakdown in the functional undergarment plan.

After I had finished, and then after I had calmed down, and then after I had calmed down the photographer and made her a cup of chamomile tea, and after we had taken some photos and after I had calmed her down again and told her not to worry, I rang my son.

I told him what the photographer had thought was going on.

'Should I be offended?' he said. 'Should you be offended? Who comes off best here?' There was a pause and then he said, 'This world can be a funny place.' And we started laughing.

6

FATHER KARMA

My son was right. This world can be a funny place. Especially when you get a touch of Father Karma. It can strike anywhere but usually it hits when you're out and about and is prompted by encountering something or someone who makes you contemplate the whole experience of fatherhood. I was struck by it on a trip to a shopping mall the size of a small planet.

It didn't help that on the day we went to the mall I received a series of phone calls before we even left the house. First from one of my agents. He'd been calling a bit, doing his best to convince me a play would be good.

'It's a good one, apparently.'

Had he seen it?

'No. But I've read it.'

And?

'While ago, pretty good.'

'Pretty good? High praise.'

'Very popular at the National.'

As in England's National Theatre. Now it's in Australia a year or two after opening on the West End or Broadway.

Actors used to bung on American or English accents in foreign plays, but mostly now they use Australian accents. Whether that's good or bad I don't know. It might be nice if more Australian plays were done. Apparently, they're not that popular.

Nothing sells like Broadway or West End on a poster. Just the way things are.

Supposed to be a good play. About clinical studies into anti-depressants and the idea of love between people.

The agent had rung a lot. 'What do you think, Will?'

'Jesus, that sounds like a rib-tickler,' is my first opinion.

'No, no, it's very good.'

'I don't know, I'll have a think.'

'You said that last time.'

I know.

'I'll ring you,' says the agent.

Okay.

A bit later, it's raining. I sit on the verandah, look out at the rain and pat my dogs.

Phone call.

Not the agent. Not even from Australia.

Somebody from a call centre was calling about an opportunity that shouldn't be missed. The line wasn't very good. I had to yell.

The dogs cringed a bit.

I patted them.

Did I want a golden opportunity to lower something, my costs?

'Sorry?' I said.

'It's a good offer.'

He sounded like my agent. I let whoever it was say whatever they say haltingly.

A pause.

He's finished his spiel.

The pause continues.

'What's the weather like where you are?' I shout.

Another pause. 'It's hot, very hot. What is the weather like for you?'

'Wet, very wet,' I say.

'Are you working? In the rain?' he asks.

'No, no. I'm waiting for my kids to come home and then we're going shopping.'

There is a pause.

'We're buying shoes, they both need shoes.'

'Shoes are important,' says the voice from the call centre.

'Yes, we're going up to Highpoint,' I say, as if this fellow will know the shopping centre up the road.

'My daughter loves shopping . . . too much!' says the man. 'I like to spoil her.'

'Good,' I yell.

'Do you have a daughter?'

'I do.'

'Spoil her!' he laughs. 'They grow up fast. It is very hot here.'

'Righto,' I say and then there is no more small talk. 'Well, good luck to you.'

'And good luck to you . . . and your shopping trip.'

'Thanks for calling.'

'That is all right,' and he hangs up.

I tap.

Phone call. Another call centre, closer to home, Sydney, I'm guessing, but with a voice just as foreign, a spruiker for a charity I donate to, asking for a further donation. A cheeky chappy o'right mate English person talking about disaster victims but sounding like he's selling a vacuum cleaner.

'Ello Willyam, can I call you Willyam or Will? Wotcha prefer?'

I tell him it doesn't matter.

'Well, Will, sure you've heard 'bout the awful tragedy, 'bout de earfquake. One of the worst, horrendous. Now I can see you've been a supporter for some time now, so fanks so much for ya ongoin' support, really 'preciated. Very much so, but I'm sure you'd 'gree that the families who 'ave suffered as cons'quence of de earfquake need all the 'elp we can give. So we're 'oping you can maybe give an extra one-off donation to 'elp.'

What am I going to say? No?

I top up my donation amount.

'Fanks, Will.'

I ask if he has seen a play at the National Theatre about anti-depressants and clinical studies and love.

'Featre? No, mate, like the telly myself.'

I say goodbye.

He says ta-ta.

Then, after the kids are home and we are heading off to the retail planet known as Highpoint in Maribyrnong, there is another phone call. My old mate PB from Redcliffe, the town where we both grew up.

'What's news?' I ask. PB's been to Sutton Street, to Cliff Hanan – *the* jeweller.

I laugh.

Cliff was a big believer in Val Morgan cinema advertising and was known as *the* jeweller courtesy of Val's work. As if he was the only jeweller that ever existed.

Val Morgan still exists today, all flashy digital ads and big music as it proclaims itself to whoever is in the cinema watching the pre-feature trailers and ads. But alongside its flashier national advertisements there were also regional efforts which were geographically specific. These had a homemade slide-show night feel to them with a big-voiced voiceover man adding a seemingly incongruous element to the whole effort.

As teenagers PB and I would go to see the flicks at Redcliffe Entertainment Centre and we'd sit through a couple of big-budget efforts from tobacco companies, like a Peter Stuyvesant Passport to Smoking Pleasure or House of Dunhill advertisements complete with lots of locations and beautiful people doing things that beautiful people do when they were allowed to flog ciggies. Such as the Alpine ad with two beautiful people, a woman and a man, in flowing white linen, fake tans, with flowing blond hair riding white horses more beautiful even than them, with manes even more flowing than the humans' hair, all to the strains of big beautiful music.

Then we'd have a slide, sometimes back to front, for Cliff Hanan, *the* jeweller.

'How is Cliff the jeweller?' I ask.

'He's given it away; it's now Lester Hanan *the* jeweller.'

'That's his son, is it?' I ask.

'Oh yes,' assures PB. 'But he's kept the Cliff title though; saves on signage and keeps things familiar for folk. A bit like The Phantom, you know how the sons always take over the role. And so, people think he's immortal.'

'That is a big call on *the* jeweller. An immortal there in the arcades.'

'Well, maybe he's like all those popes called Clement. Different blokes but they took the name, so you choose, pontiff or Phantom?'

'Definitely Phantom, I think.'

'You know you're right. It's the. The Phantom. The jeweller. Anyway, I paid him a visit.'

'Did you, how was he?'

'*The* jeweller passed on a bit of news from the universe of Redcliffe's shopping precinct and the latest departure from Redcliffe's long dark arcades is a shock. Uncle Boots.'

'Oh . . . really?' My son looks at me with concern, it's the tone in my voice.

'Was he a mate of yours?' he asks.

PB and I laugh. 'No, no he was just a bloke,' I say.

My son shakes his head a little.

•

Uncle Boots was just some bloke who also happened to be a key cutter and boot repairer. He'd been hovering in the middle of the arcade for years in his red working jacket. He had a big handlebar mo and black hair parted in the middle that hung near to his shoulders. A bit of a bass guitarist in a rock band look, not a glam or pop band but a rock band.

'Clean anything from your boots except for chewy and dog turds,' he would say when customers asked if he might be able to help with their shoes.

'Now he's gone,' says PB a little wistfully.

Redcliffe has that effect. I feel a twinge.

'Closed up because no one was interested in learning the trade, according to *the* jeweller. Cliff told me Uncle

Boots tried to get his kids interested but they weren't up for it, apparently. So he pulled the plug.'

I remembered a dinner when I was home from uni on holidays. It was around the time my old man was thinking of selling his business. 'Might as well try and flog it,' he said at the table, 'Not much chance it'd stay in the family.'

I told my father I didn't know about that.

My father looked at me and then asked slowly, 'You serious?'

I nodded my head and then laughed. 'Of course not!'

My father laughed a little too. Why would any of us kids be interested?

But I noticed he sat very still for a while.

I thought perhaps I should say sorry, but then he started up again with his dinner.

After a break in the conversation about politics and how tasty the chops were, I started to say I hadn't meant anything but he stopped me. He held up his hand as he reached for a bottle of HP sauce.

'Not to worry, son, just shush, it doesn't matter.' And he gave a little thumbs up even though he didn't look at me.

It didn't matter.

But it probably had. Why wouldn't it? That hire equipment business of my father's may have been mostly handmade and modest but he had made it. He was thinking of selling it, and that meant his life was closing down a little; he loved working and being busy. He was surrendering to time and here was his youngest son making a joke out of the business that had fed and provided for me and the rest of my family.

My father had been happy being his own man, building his houses and tooling around the streets of the peninsula and surrounds, delivering whatever people had wanted to hire.

And I had laughed at it and him.

All these years later, I wince at the memory of my father sitting still and quiet after I had laughed.

Then, like an idiot, I wondered if one of the Phantoms ever sat down at dinner and wondered out loud if any of his sons were interested in going into the family business, and how he would have felt sitting there at the table with his chops and HP sauce, a serviette tucked into his purple jumpsuit, when his youngest son laughed.

It was sort of funny but sort of sad.

•

I am silent as I drive the car slowly up to the upper level of the Highpoint shopping planet carpark.

'It's raining, Dad,' says my son.

'No kidding.'

'We'll get soaked,' says my daughter.

'We'll get a park,' I mutter. 'It'll be packed downstairs.'

My son says we should have gone shopping online. It's raining quite heavily.

'Well, if you wanted to do that you should have done it before you needed your boots tomorrow. Made time for them to post it to you.'

My son laughs a little. 'Like you know about online shopping.'

My daughter snorts.

'You bought any more of your big-nosed fishing hats, Big Fella?' says my son.

I turn my big-beaked, big-nose special fishing cap, of which I had inadvertently ordered twenty when I thought I was only purchasing two online, and tell him to shut up.

He smiles and shakes his head.

We sit in the car until the rain has lessened enough for us to get out and chance the weather.

We laugh the way you do sometimes when you run in the rain, a bit of fun that takes you out of yourself.

And then inside the shopping planet, I can feel the weight of the humanity. The place is packed and streams of people slowly make their way along with no discernible intent, moving with the same rhythm. The heating is turned up in the manner shopping centres insist on having, adding to the closeness pressing down on us.

It's as if the shopping planet has a heavier atmosphere than Earth, and we begin to move in the same leaden way.

Somebody says hello to me. I turn and say hello back. Both my kids groan. It's a young woman, maybe the same age as my son, perhaps a little older. She is dressed in black and has, I think, a Scandinavian accent.

As soon as I see her I groan as well. She is a spruiker for some kind of hand cream. I've stopped now, it seems easier to just stand rather than try and re-enter the stream of shoppers. I listen to her bang on about Dead Sea Salt moisturising cream.

Am I familiar with the Dead Sea? Am I aware of the unique properties of its salt extracted by a unique method which means the unique qualities remain concentrated in a perfume-free unique moisturising cream?

Would I like to try a sample? Would I care to purchase a gift pack perhaps, already wrapped and ready to go?

I hold my hand up and am about to say no thanks when I hear myself say, 'I'll just take a tub thanks, no gift pack.'

She stops, looks a bit surprised and then says great. And I get out my card to pay.

My children stare, shake their heads and wait.

I ask the young woman where she is from. She says Denmark, and I assume she is on a working holiday.

She is, six months into a year-long visit.

'Enjoying yourself?'

'Yeah,' she says. 'Are you sure you don't want a gift pack?'

'I'm certain, thanks.'

'Okay, just making sure.' She puts the tub of Dead Sea Salt into a bag and gives it to me. 'It's a little bit of a drag to be in here today but, you know, it's money! Have a nice day.'

I move off with my kids.

'Why did you buy that?' says my daughter.

'Why did you even stop?' says my son. 'The only people who say hello to you in shopping centres are the people who want to sell you crap or charity spruikers.'

I knew this. Not far away was a charity stall with people singing out in vain to people as they drifted past. And I knew that the tub of Dead Sea Salt was probably about as unique as a tub of margarine but I bought it anyway.

I shrug my shoulders. I think I know why I bought it. Father Karma. There in the shopping planet, I felt that wretched feeling that any person can get when they have spent enough time wandering around this world.

Most parents get it, I am sure, and it always makes you feel rather tiny and even shabby.

It's Life, with all its uncertainties and unfairness. And it hits me in the shopping planet that my son was right – the world can be a funny place. More than a funny place sometimes. A wretched dark and lonely place. A place where somebody can find themselves a long way from home. Even in a shopping mall.

I think of the phone calls.

Of the bloke in that call centre where it is so very hot who likes to spoil his daughter too much when he takes her shopping, the cheeky chappy charity man banging on about the earthquake victims. Thousands killed because they live in a particular place where dreadful natural disasters occur, one of the endless Third World countries where epically awful things seem to happen, images of which are flashed upon your TV screen in between whatever you are watching. The sort of place where you can't turn the temperature up or down as you may like. And you stand in the shopping planet thinking what a patronising arse you are to think like that, but then another part of you thinks why wouldn't you think like that; after all, you come from the sort of place which produces a theatrical piece of entertainment about mental health and clinical trials and ideas of love.

Entitled?

In short, I'm a middle-aged middle-class man indulging in a ten-minute attack of the guilts. Father Karma.

That's why I bought the tub of unique Dead Sea Salt, because some young person with English as a second language who is about as far away from her family as she could get is flogging it to make a bit of money.

I see her and think, what if my kids were over the other side of the world trying to earn a few dollars? Would anybody stop for them? I'd like to think that there might be some foreign version of myself rustling about in his pockets for some money who might even take the time to chat with them.

It makes no sense though and a part of me knows it. I look at the two people I care most about in the world, my children, who are looking back at me rather disdainfully, as if I'm a large mound of human hassle.

It's too hard to try and verbalise how I feel and I wonder if they know what I'm thinking.

It's that part of you wanting life to be good for your children but knowing that you can't stop life happening, you can't stop the way your kids will grow and change and live. They can't stay as little toddlers that cling to you, listen to your words as if you were the one who knew best.

Or maybe my son could stay that little boy who chased after butterflies in the backyard and gently caught them in his little hands and then let them go with a little laugh. Or always be that little boy who could hardly wait for a *Star Wars* movie and in his excitement would say over and over again that he couldn't wait to see 'Esipode the one'.

Or perhaps my daughter could remain as that funny little girl who would skip with her big sunhat along the footpath on her way to school like an animated mushroom singing as she went, 'I love living!'

But then she wouldn't grow up to be that lovely sixteen-year-old who held my hand on a flight to Japan when turbulence hit and shook the plane so badly people screamed.

Not being a very good flyer at the best of times, I had recently started to vocalise my reactions to the rather unpleasant experience of bumps in the air.

I wasn't much good at science at school but had a basic enough grasp of physics and the effects of gravity that I never quite felt comfortable with the whole concept of a heavy object like a large commercial airliner, with an almost equally heavy object like me on board, travelling through the air.

My experience wasn't helped when I admitted to a fellow passenger once in a lounge why I didn't like flying that much. He, it turned out, was a science teacher.

'Look,' he said as I helped myself to another liquid sedative from the bar, 'if it helps you any, with all the elements of thrust and weight to power ratio, it is the case, really, not so much of flying but of controlled falling.'

He smiled as if he had given me a gift. I felt like strangling him. How on earth could I come to terms with the idea of controlled falling?

He smiled a little more, nodded and held out his palms and looked like a TV make-believe father, say in the manner of Fred MacMurray having a chat with his problematical middle son, Robbie.

Perhaps he could even sell his pithy little explanation to the airlines? 'Come fall with us' or 'Fall away to your ideal holiday', 'Falling in comfort'.

So, no, I wasn't a good flyer and when even a slight tremble moved through the aircraft I emitted not howls or screams but something even worse: 'father exclamations'.

'Hey, come on now!' or 'Not on, not good enough!' or 'What are you up to?' Almost as if the pilots were naughty children who were mucking around and doing something to the aircraft to make it shudder.

'Do I have to get out of my seat?' or 'Do you want us to stop the plane?' were almost on the tip of my tongue. I have no idea why I started doing this, but perhaps it was because I had let rip with a barrage of swearing when a plane bumped about a little too willingly on a journey to Perth.

I spent the rest of the flight – sorry, fall – and my trip to the luggage carousel to collect my bags apologising for my language.

On that trip to Japan, the plane shook, buffeted by the air, and I was very frightened and then I felt my hand being held by my daughter and I turned to her and she just smiled.

There was a bit more shaking and one big bump and a quiet moment where everybody held their collective breath.

Then there was stillness. And then my daughter, myself and the rest of the passengers in our proximity laughed.

•

That sixteen-year-old version of my daughter may not have totally solved my falling dislike, but she made me feel a little safer and like I mattered.

So, standing in the shopping planet, I ask myself which version of my children to keep?

My son flicks his hand at me to say, Come on, let's go. I nod my head and we walk off, rejoining the stream of shoppers. We manage to make it to a shoe shop.

The shop is busy, with quite a few of what I take to be fellow travellers, people out for school shoes like my daughter. I look at them, young adults accompanied by one or other of their parents, bored a little by having to be here, probably with better things to do, paying little heed to a Father Karma moment when life's fragility and chance plays about a father's mind.

It's a bore but you also want to shake them all by their shoulders and give them the 'I've been there before' talk. At my daughter's school the other night was a parent information evening where we heard how the school was going to hopefully shepherd our daughters through their final year of high school.

I saw parents in the audience I remembered from my daughter's first days at the school and I felt that all too familiar dull thud of recognition. They were all looking old.

I could only guess what they thought when they saw me. I soon found out.

A very effusive psychologist was introduced and she began to spruik the program developed for positive parenting. She was going to give a few brief hints on how we parents, and fathers in particular, could help our daughters along the way.

These things all seem okay when somebody says them in a PowerPoint talk; things like remembering that a girl's first port of call when dealing with male relationships is most likely going to be her father. As her father, you play a large part in what a respectful and appropriate male response to life sounds and feels like.

And a twist on a chestnut, fathers, when you listen, try not to head towards 'an event of problem-solving focus' because often your daughter will try to communicate through a need to share, not problem fix.

Great, I thought, remembering all the times I had been in some grump or took the mickey out of people and threw generalisations like hand grenades, or handed on mad McInnes family traditions like never trusting anybody without lobes to their ears, or never having anything to do with anything connected to the number eighty-seven, always making sure you stared unblinking into a person's eyes when you raised a glass at a toast or even making sure you never walked between a couple because you would take their luck – good or bad – with you and never, ever writing in red ink.

All these I would have handed to my daughter as her first introduction to a male role model.

And as for listening and problem solving, I had a talent for jumping to wrong conclusions and trying to second-guess where a story would end or also just mishearing things.

Then the psychologist asked us to open the booklet we'd collected on the way in and then take a pen, turn to the person next to ourselves and draw a picture of that person. What this had to do with anything was beyond me but I dutifully turned to the man sitting alongside me.

He was a fellow I had nodded to over the years at school functions. Parent–teacher nights. Sports carnivals, a school ball and, occasionally, when we were picking up or dropping off our kids. He was an all right bloke, I supposed, who'd recently undergone a bit of a renovation. His thinning hair had flourished into something that resembled a large furry piece of marsupial road kill.

Well, good on him. But what to do? Should I incorporate the fuzz that sat atop his scalp into my picture? Would he want me to acknowledge this renovation?

I thought it would be better to just draw a smiley stick figure.

We were asked by the psychologist to show each other our efforts.

Now the point is, there's often a difference in the way you see yourself as opposed to how others see you.

And this was never more apparent to me than by what my renovated scalp friend showed me.

He had chosen the stick-figure style too, but he'd added a large beaky nose, a pair of what looked like welding goggles for glasses, an avocado-shaped midriff and, of all things, spiky shredded hair, like a badly grassed yard.

I looked at my 'portrait' and then back at him. He smiled.

'I just thought I should try to be as honest as I could,' he said.

I nodded.

'Now, how does that make you feel?' asked the psychologist. 'Happy or frustrated that you only achieved those results in the short time I gave you? Uncomfortable because you were asked to do something out of your comfort zone?'

It made me wish I had gone all out on a tribute to the possum rug he had spent a small fortune on placing on top of his melon.

'Imagine what your daughter will feel like this year because she will be challenged by this year and its tasks. Try to imagine some of the things she might feel when she looks at herself in the mirror of a morning. When she sees an image of herself from how other people might see her.'

Then I thought of Malcolm Turnbull, who apparently had thought a portrait of himself by the Archibald Prize winner Lewis Miller rather poor, reportedly describing the effort as making him look like a big, fat greedy orifice of the female gender.

The artist was so affected that he destroyed the portrait.

This was back in the early 1990s when the future PM was a very successful merchant banker and, it seems, just as effective in communicating his feelings as he is today.

It's a strange thing though, reacting to how others see you. Lewis Miller is a terrific painter and on the walls of our home is a sketch he did of my son as a young boy playing tennis. I've always thought it lovely but Malcolm's reaction to his portrait was different.

That's not unusual. Rembrandt had a portrait slashed by unhappy customers and Bill Dobell's famous Archibald prize-winning portrait of Joshua Smith was one of the great controversies in Australian art.

And now here was another. The Parent Information Night Controversy.

How did I feel? Well, no harm done. Other people's eyes tell them what they see. But I couldn't help letting my eyes drift to the marsupial mat on top of my artist's head and then drop back to meet his gaze.

Satisfyingly, he blushed. And I left it there.

Looking around the shoe shop, I think again about the psychologist's PowerPoint talk. Had I thought about how my daughter would have felt? How any of these young people on the crest of being adults would feel?

Most of the kids in the shoe shop probably have better things to do than hear a father bang on about life. But in my Father Karma state, I feel like telling them a few things.

Finishing school is a milestone. Some students can't wait to finish, some may be a little worried they'll miss the structure and order of school, and some may genuinely not care at all. But leaving high school is a big step, for the world's a lot bigger than the confines of school. Some may have it all worked out and know exactly where they're bound, what university course or trade or job they'll head into.

But sometimes life doesn't care what people may have worked out. The university course you want may elude you, the job you think you'll have may disappear or when you get there you may find that it isn't what you want.

Life is like that.

People will ask 'What are you going to do with yourself?' and you'll get sick of that question.

Your parents may badger you and begin to annoy but that is almost certainly because they want the best for you.

But there's the thing, what's the best?

The people who love you just want you to be safe and healthy and mostly happy. But that's never guaranteed, and that's why sometimes they worry. And there'll be a lot of things for people like your parents to worry about.

You driving off in a car with friends will set hearts racing.

So, if they hug for a little too long sometimes, let them, and remember it's better than them asking, 'What are you going to do with yourself?'

People are encouraged to be the best, to excel, be better than the next person.

People are told life's a competition and achieving in that competition defines you. To follow your dreams and never take a backward step. Well, take it from me, while that may be the plot of some entertaining sports movie from the 1990s, that's not life. Sooner or later you will find out that not all dreams come true, no matter how much you try to follow them, and no matter how hard you compete, there may well be someone who is better.

That's life.

There'll be times when life will rub you the wrong way, you'll discover what broken hearts and dashed hopes and just missing out really mean.

The longer you live, the more acute time will become and there'll be times life will hurt. There'll be bruises and scrapes. It's best to realise learning from life isn't compromising. That cutting people a bit of slack and leaving a bit of space for others isn't backing down or not competing, it's growing up and being a citizen of the world.

And that is a pretty good thing to be.

And remember, sometimes you may find yourself in a place where you think nobody has ever been. That nobody has ever been so alone as you may feel. That you can't step back.

But believe me, you can. Somebody has been there before and there is almost always a way back from a precipice.

Just a few words of advice. I feel like grabbing the shopping planet's PA system and asking, 'Now, by the way — what are you going to do with yourself?'

•

My daughter is turning seventeen. I can barely believe it. Time is going by and she is growing up and that, I suppose, is that. Like so many homes, ours is plastered with lots of photos from the past. Snatches of frozen time.

Their subjects have changed.

There's a photo of me holding my son upside down at the beach, him aged three and laughing with his big smile.

He is twenty-one now, a big lovely Clydesdale of a young man. I couldn't lift him a centimetre if I tried, but he still has his big lovely smile.

And there's photos of my wife holding my daughter, they both have the same eyes. Smiling but watchful.

My wife is dead and my daughter is turning seventeen. Her eyes are still smiling and watchful. Now people say how my daughter reminds them of her mother.

I worry.

Perhaps it's because I am a single parent and a man and a conservative old fart, but I look at my daughter and I worry.

I feel a bit of a dullard when I ask myself 'Why is it so much harder for a woman in this world?' My mother answered this for me once when I told her the world could be unfair.

'Well, you lot made it, by and large, so live with it – you middle-aged, over-educated, overweight white men!'

And I know being a young man these days is more complex than when I was a young fellow and, even though

I worry, somehow, I just think my big gorgeous Clydesdale will muddle through. I watch him find the Blundstone boots he was after and sit waiting while my daughter contemplates a pair of runners to go with her school shoes.

My daughter – how will she fare?

It seems to be a different world out there for women.

They don't get paid as much as men. There seems to be so many more expectations on what a woman must look like as opposed to what the content of her character may be.

If women want a career as well as a family then they want everything, if a woman doesn't have a family and has a career it's her own choice.

I don't know. It just seems lately that women who stick their heads up above the trenches of life seem to get them kicked a bit more willingly.

I think about the scenes from the previous night's television news, about Professor Gillian Triggs, the former President of the Human Rights Commission, and the Report into Children in Detention and the way she was hectored and bullied before a Senate Review Committee wasn't a great look.

There are extreme examples of how difficult life can be for women, even in a country as blessed and as privileged as Australia.

One only has to look to the former Australian of the Year, Rosie Batty, for proof of that particular point.

And there are also the more mundane, everyday hurdles and barriers that women, including my daughter, have to deal with – even hearing people being called 'a girl' as a term of abuse. And then there's stereotypes ridiculed by the *Forbes* business magazine in an article about how 'powerful women' are characterised. When men get angry it's seen as a sign of status but in women it's seen as a lack of competence. Or if a man achieves a role of significance it's taken as an earned achievement but when a woman manages to sit in a position of power it's seen as an accident or tokenism.

And, being a boofhead, I wondered if The Phantom ever asked any of his daughters if they wanted to take over the family business of being the jungle dude dressed in purple. Why couldn't a girl be allowed to dress up in a silly costume and go fight evil and be brave? Why even in a make-believe comic strip did a girl have to mentally jump gender to be allowed to be a hero?

And I remember whose daughter she is. Who her mother was, a woman with kind and watchful eyes and more strength of character and determination than anybody I have ever known.

And I think this world is changing, maybe slowly, but it is changing.

I just wish I didn't worry.

And there it is. I'm a father, I think to myself, who's had a trip not just to the shopping planet but to the state of Worry, and I know I'll always worry, not all the time, but it'll be there just below the surface, ready to bubble away.

Then my son laughs and my daughter shakes her head.

'He's got that look, hasn't he?' says my son.

My daughter looks at me.

'What look?' I ask.

'That look you've had since you were on the phone to PB.'

'What look?'

'The look where you frown and sigh every so often and then grind your teeth,' says my daughter. 'And you stare and make that sucking sound with your mouth.'

I just stare back. And grind my teeth and make a sucking sound with my mouth.

I stop.

'The look which means you're either going to yell at us or tell us that you love us,' says my daughter. 'That Dad look thing.'

I stare back at them.

'Look, Dad, do not worry. Maybe old Uncle Boots is kicking back and chilling. Maybe that crap you bought from that girl with the accent is unique, although I don't think it is, but it's nice you stopped and bought it.'

'But just don't worry,' says my daughter and then, after a pause, she continues, 'so much.'

The phone rings. It's the agent.

He'll want to know whether I have any thoughts about the play. I let it ring out. I'll call him back. I'm out with people I care about.

I look at my kids and tell them I love them. I can't help myself, really.

They just shake their heads.

They know me a little too well and I must admit that's quite nice.

A LETTER TO MY SON

The year before my son finished high school, he went on a Year 11 retreat, a time of reflection. The boys were given a letter written to them by their parents that they would read and reflect upon. This is the letter my son received from his father.

Dear Clem,

This is your real father. And I think you have done him proud.

Okay it's not your real father, although sometimes I suppose you would like a man like him to be your father. And I can understand that. I mean, who wouldn't? He has sacrificed his head hair to spread it around his body instead. He knows the meaning of asset management.

Look, Clem, I think you could learn a lot from him. How to present well for job interviews, and also

how to go about making the world a better place.
But, sadly, he is not your father.

This man is your father.

No, no. No, he's not your father either.

I am your father. Yes me – farting, growling yelling hack William McInnes. And let me tell you, I couldn't be prouder.

You are Clem and that is someone who I love. But you are also someone I like. Really like ... most of the time. All right, enough bad humour. You are a good man-child. A good bloke-ette. And, most importantly, a good man.

Yes, you are. The force is strong in you as the farts are strong in me.

Stop it.

I held you just after you were born for what I thought was a couple of minutes. It turned out to be nearly an hour. I just looked at you and thought that you were the best and loveliest thing I had ever held or seen.

I look at you now and - all right it's not all the time - but I still feel the same way.

Yes, you can be lazy and you lie (give that up, mate, you are a worse liar than me and I am appalling) and you eat a bit too much junk and drink too much of those crappy energy drinks but you are someone with compassion and fairness and a lot of love in you and that, to me, is the most important thing to have in life.

You aren't, and won't, always be a super saint, but you are fundamentally a good man and you have already made this world a better place. Keep going.

Keep growing. Be yourself and live. By doing that you'll continue to make the world good.

You have made me, and your two other fathers pictured above, proud and annoyed, happy and grumpy but above all you have made me feel a love that has made me a better person. So thank you.

I love you, Clem. I'm proud of you and I like you. Now clean your fucking room, study until your brain aches and don't eat with your mouth open. I never understood how you could actually eat with your mouth closed but – hang on, I get it, it's chew. Don't chew with your mouth open.

Be nice with people, because you are going to be a big good-looking fellow.

So that's it.

Wait, there's more. You, Doug and I used to go walking around that West Footscray footy oval when you were just a baby. Early in the morning. For quite a long time. I carried you in a sling, and you used to hang about me.

I have never failed to feel happy and warm whenever I think of those times. I even rested a pie I bought from the Barkly Street Bakery on your head and then forgot I put it there and got into a flap because I wanted to eat it and couldn't find it. We walked around for about an hour with you wearing a pie on your head.

I know I'm a boofhead but I love you. Good on you, Clemmy, and thank you.

Your Third Dad,
William McInnes.

Your Second Dad,
Lord Vader.

Your First Dad,
Bevan Krunt.

7

FATHER KNOWS BEST

I once sat on a writers' festival panel with five authors and a breathless moderator who introduced us. In the breathless moderator's words, one author was a writer of important and serious works, one was a debut author who had made an impressive start to what she felt sure would be an impressive career, and so on and so on, and the last author – me – was described as 'quite popular'.

It's nice to know where you fit in the scheme of things.

The writer of serious and important works had a very serious and important air about him as he spoke about his thoughts on families. I must admit I didn't quite catch what it was he was saying about families but he did have a serious list of names who'd written books.

'As Nabokov said, I think it was Proust, Graham Greene suggested, Dickens had it half right, Tolstoy – poor deluded Tolstoy – stated, Hemingway declared of course and Joyce intimated.'

Well, Joyce could have intimated about the double from Doomben for all I knew and Tolstoy, poor deluded Tolstoy, could have been giving household cleaning tips: '*Nyet, nyet, nyet,* you should never, ever microwave your cleaning sponge.'

But the serious and important author was impressive. People nodded and the breathless moderator was suitably breathless. And then the author drew a round of applause when he stopped, took a deep breath and said slowly, 'It wasn't until the birth of my third child, after I had held this little human aloft in my arms, that I thought, perhaps life is no longer about me. Perhaps.'

I thought to myself how a man with a brain the size of a planet could only get an inkling that life was not about him anymore with child number three. It had taken him that long? His third child? I mean, the whole thing about becoming a father is that life is no longer really about you anymore. Even Marlin Perkins from *Wild Kingdom* had that one worked out.

I made a mental note to avoid the serious and important writer in the festival's very well-stocked green room. No good wasting a gargle with somebody who'd just list dead people and a few of their words.

But the serious and important writer hadn't finished. He then said he gave his child the most important advice he could think of: 'I held this little life form, told this little life form, told my child to . . . *breathe* . . . Breathe in all of life that you can.'

He drew another round of applause with that one and I thought, good luck to him, he's just trying to flog some books. He sounded a little bit like what I imagine Moses would have been like, or maybe somebody playing Moses, say Charlton Heston during his mid-toupee years.

Breathe.

I thought of what I said when I had held my newborn children. 'Hello there, you,' I think was about the size of it.

Although I did remember being incredibly impressed with my son when I was changing one of his first nappies and he was staring at me with eyes that seemed to be thinking about something very hard.

I stared back. And then he peed, a stream of pee that arced up in the air and landed over his head. Not a drop touched him.

'Oh, you legend! Leave a little bit of life in the tank, you don't want to peak too early. But, undeniably impressive.'

I was definitely more boofhead than name-dropping Moses, but I realised we were both trying to say the same thing. My own father would put it this way: 'Have a crack at life, a real crack, but just remember to leave a little space for other folk.'

Fathers giving advice and trying to pass things on to their offspring, or little life forms if you're Moses the serious and important writer, can be one of life's little adventures. The trick is not falling into the Polonius Syndrome where what you say isn't necessarily what you yourself do or even believe.

Polonius is a character from Shakespeare's *Hamlet*, who happens to be an adviser to King Claudius, who had bumped off Hamlet's dad and married Hamlet's mother. Polonius is also the father of Ophelia, who is Hamlet's intended squeeze, and Laertes, who is a pal of Hamlet's. Laertes is one of those plot devices who is just there to move the action along or be a sounding board for another character to spout at. And Polonius can spout plenty, as is seen in the famous speech he gives his son/plot device

Laertes as the son is about to depart to France and his adult life.

In plain boofhead language, Polonius gives his son a series of rules for living a good life as a man. Don't say what you think, and don't be too quick to act on what you think, be friendly but not too friendly, once you have tested a friendship and it's proven true then hold onto that friendship, don't be too quick to get into a fight but if you are in one put on a show, hear everyone's opinion but keep your own to yourself, if you're going to get clothes make them good because clothes make the man. Don't borrow or lend money. Don't lend it to a friend because you'll lose that friendship and borrowing money makes one a spendthrift. Be true to yourself and by doing that you won't be false to anybody else.

Now the great thing about Polonius is that he is a blowhard and a gossip and his advice is all for nothing, for his son's fate, and that of almost everybody else in *Hamlet*, heads south very quickly.

Polonius gets stabbed by Hamlet while he's hiding behind a curtain spying on Hamlet and Queen Gertrude, Hamlet's mother.

And then Ophelia goes mad and ends up drowned, King Claudius is stabbed by Hamlet, Gertrude drinks poison that was meant for Hamlet and Laertes is killed by Hamlet. And then Hamlet dies. Bravo, end of show.

So, in the pantheon of dud advice from a father, Polonius is right up there.

And yet it's a list that is often quoted as advice for young men, which seems crazy to me because it sounds like some ranting radio shock jock or maybe a wish list for some extremist political party holding an Ayn Rand fancy dress night.

Keep mum about what you believe in, look good, keep your money to yourself, don't let on what you are really thinking and if you get into a fight, get in and go hard. Don't lend money and remain true to number one – you.

There was a father of a girl I was desperate to go out with who would quote some of these lines, or the substantive meaning of them, to his children.

He ended up in jail for embezzlement.

So, watch out for the Polonius Syndrome when you're giving advice. It could come back to haunt you.

I remember not too long after the father–son glove night at the Redcliffe Police Citizens Youth Club, my father called me over behind one of his trucks and gave me a bit of advice.

'If you ever find yourself in a fight, and you want to get out of it quick, punch whoever is in front of you right on the nose or kick the fella in the ankles. Right.'

I nodded.

'But only in a fight, okay?'

I nodded.

'Just thought you should know that, might come in handy.'

I looked up at him, a big brown man, bare-chested and holding a paintbrush. I could smell what he'd been working with – an almost mythical substance called creosote. This stuff, which was a by-product from the distillation of tars and was used as a preserving agent on timber, was beloved by my father. He would slap it on any piece of timber he had lying around that he thought could be useful in any form of building.

It was black and oily and had the smoky smell of freshly laid bitumen.

He looked down at me and then held up the brush dripping with creosote. 'Would you like to know how to use this stuff? I tell you, if you could drink it you'd be healthier than Charles Atlas.'

I'd had, I thought, enough advice from my father. I made a face and backed off a few steps.

My old man nodded. 'Righto then,' and he patted me on the head and went back to splashing the creosote on the wood. I don't know why he decided to pass on his advice about where to thump somebody, perhaps preserving the wood with his miraculous creosote was quite meditative and he was just having a think about things.

But years later, at a pub in Townsville, an almighty blue broke out and I found myself in the middle of it, getting a proper quilting from a fellow I had never seen before in my life. I had no idea who or what started the fight but I just knew I had landed in it on the way to the bar to shout a round.

From above the din, I remembered my father's words and somehow managed to snot my energetic attacker on his snout and to my great relief he staggered back with tears forming in his eyes. I chivalrously decided not to take advantage of his incapacitated state and lit off, giving my old man a nod of thanks.

His advice had worked. In a situation not of my making, I had made it away roughly in one piece. It was, as advice goes, a bit old school but I thought when my young son and I were out fishing one Sunday afternoon that I should pass it on to him.

He was about the same age as I had been when my father told me his self-preservation trick. I thought it would just hang about in my son's mind somewhere, to be pulled out and put into practice if the situation required.

No.

A few days after my advice, I was called into the classroom by my son's teacher to have a little chat. She held a sheet of paper in front of her. 'We did a project about Father's Day.' She paused, I nodded and she went on slowly, 'And what fathers tell you.'

I had a slight sinking feeling after she showed me a drawing by a kid called Kevin of his father telling him to brush his teeth.

Another of a father and his daughter washing the dog.

And then my son's drawing of a goofy smiling man, me, pointing out how to kick another goofy smiling person in the ankles – in fact, there were quite a few goofy smiling people getting hit or kicked.

'Well, at least everyone seems happy,' I said, trying to make light of the situation.

The teacher just stared and I had an awkward ten minutes explaining the background of my fatherly advice.

•

Some advice and knowledge fathers attempt to hand down has no foundation in first-hand experience. Take fathers trying to teach their children the ways of sport. I have sat on the sidelines of training sessions and games of kids' sport enough to realise that a lot of what a father tells his offspring isn't always grounded in anything to do with that rather key element in the passing on of any type of knowledge, namely having some minor grasp of what you are talking about.

Most father sporting statements are about the opposition. 'They're not that big', 'not that fast', 'not that tough', 'not that skilled' but it's the 'not that big' brushoff that makes no sense.

If you are a kid and see a bigger kid lining up against you then of course the size of the opposition is one of the first things you notice.

It's basic biology 101. I recognise a potential threat, I better watch out, but wait, no, don't worry about that because here is your father banging on about the threat not being that big.

Being told by some grown-up that 'They're not that big' gives no comfort to anybody, because the first thing a kid thinks when they hear it is, 'Yes, well, maybe not to you, you're a grown-up.' It is a stark lesson in relativity, especially when the grown-up may well be holding a coffee and rugged up in comfort on the sidelines.

Sometimes 'advice' is just a lie. 'No, your uniforms look great. Tuck your jersey in your shorts and pull your socks up and you'll run faster.'

On what scientific formula is that one worked out?

On the sidelines before one of my daughter's netball matches, a father of one of the girls was asked to stand in as coach because the mother who was the usual coach had been held up at work. She thought this father might be suitable because he was sporty. He was also slightly deluded.

'Girls,' he clapped his hands. 'Gather round.'

Ten fourteen-year-olds stood in a circle.

'It's all about knowing your role, knowing your plan and knowing who to support. Knowing who to target, knowing where to pass the ball. You're a team but you've got to know how to use your assets. What are your assets?'

The girls stood there.

'Kim! Kim's your asset! Use Kim! Throw the ball to Kim,' he enthused, as if he had just shown this little gang of teenagers the way to glory.

Kim was this man's daughter. The poor girl's face went bright red and she stared deep into the court's black depths.

Fathers wanting desperately for their children to be good at sport isn't a new concept and the reasons are a mixture of simply wanting your child to succeed and having that success in some way validate you as a father.

Even precise sporting advice can go off on a tangent.

I can remember going for an after-lunch walk many years ago on a lovely weekend day and walking past some cricket nets where a kid and someone I took to be his father were engaging in the age-old ritual of the transference of cricketing knowledge.

The boy was wrapped up in what looked like new gear: helmet, gloves, thigh pads, brand-name bat and pads while he waddled about by the stumps swinging the bat like an axe.

'Let me slog one, let me slog.'

'Listen,' said the father. 'I'm not going to bowl to you until you hold the bat properly. It's a vertical grip. Hold the bat straight down, the bottom pointing to your feet.'

The boy groaned and stood as instructed.

'That's it,' said the father. 'You see how much bat you've got to hit the ball with? Horizontal, sideways, you've only got the width of the bat, vertically, long ways, you've got the length of the bat to belt the ball.

The kid just said, 'I can't slog it. I want to slog it. Can I slog it?'

'No, that's not the point, when you learn how not to slog then you'll be able to slog it, really slog it.'

'That doesn't make any sense,' said the boy.

'That is what cricket is all about. Learning how not to do something so you know how to do it.'

'That doesn't make sense.'

'Well, that's what cricket means.'

'I want to slog it.'

The father then made the fatal mistake of saying, 'Give me that bat and I'll show you.'

The boy threw back his head in operatic anguish and stomped off the way a young boy can and the father gave him the ball and took the bat.

He stood by the stumps. He held up the bat.

'I'll show you how to slog without slogging.'

He took a stance and held the bat vertically and swept through in a pretty fair straight drive. 'You see? You have all this area to hit the ball, and the follow-through of the bat gives it the momentum to hit the ball further without having to exert that much force. You see?'

I could see his point. I had had this lesson years before as well. Next would be the demonstration of how a cross-bat shot, say a pull or a hook, gives you only the area of the width of the bat to hit the ball, you have to be more precise and exert more effort to make a cross-bat shot count.

That's what the father did.

'You see how I have a smaller area of the bat to hit the ball? How I have to swing the bat harder? With a cross bat? A slog shot?'

The boy stood in his gear, seething. He had taken one of his batting gloves off and was holding the ball ready to throw it to his father when told.

'Now I'll show you again,' and the father demonstrated the flowing drive. 'And you throw me the ball.'

The father went on to demonstrate his cross-bat shot and then the drive again, but unfortunately as soon as his son had heard 'throw me the ball' he wound up and let rip a fair peg of the cricket ball.

The father had just finished his phantom non-slog slog straight drive and decided to hold the pose to prove a point when the shiny Kookaburra ball hit him where no man likes to be hit.

He made a wheezy deflating groan, which could only mean that he had been hit amidships in the area that I like to think the serious and important writer would term, 'that part of man from whence springs the seed of his future life form'. One could also have just advised the father to 'Breathe'.

I tried not to laugh but had to leave when I heard the boy say, 'That's not a slog,' only to be answered by another deflated groan of pain from his father who was in the process of falling to the ground in that progressive cantilevered manner that seems to occur when such strikes upon the body happen.

As for my own son and his cricket career, the best and most accurate piece of advice I ever gave him was when he was about twelve and filled in for a fourth-grade game in which I was playing. Like any kid playing against adults, he was filled with a mild dose of trepidation (the 'they're not that big' syndrome) and asked me how he should go about batting.

I was padding up myself and stopped putting on my gear to look him in the eye. I put a hand on his shoulder and said very solemnly, 'Don't do what I do.'

Which was basically go the tonk and hold the bat like it was a pitchfork in the hands of a crazed villager off to visit Dr Frankenstein and his monster. My preferred method was to swing like a dunny door in a cyclone.

My son turned out to be quite a proficient cricketer, and I like to think that this piece of advice helped him along the way.

Certainly, it is an example of little life forms learning from their father by simply watching how he goes about the business of life.

Take my daughter, who came to me not that long ago and asked if I could mend a picture frame she liked. Why she thought someone with my history of manual arts disasters would be able to mend the frame is a triumph of a daughter's love for her father over logic, but nonetheless I think she learned a valuable lesson.

She said that she had been researching it on the internet and just wanted to check a few things with me. I held up my hand and gave a suitably middle-aged waggle with my index finger and told her to come with me to Bunnings.

'But it said on the internet –'

I cut her off with wise father words. 'Gaffer tape or glue.'

'Dad, no gaffer tape, I want the frame to look good,' she protested. 'You always use too much gaffer tape when you fix things.'

'You know you've fixed whatever you needed to fix when you've used all the gaffer tape.'

'Dad, no gaffer tape.'

'Okay then, it's glue.'

She sighed and said okay and we sauntered off to Bunnings to join the great grazing herd of home handy-people, wandering the aisles like wildebeests plodding the plains from an old David Attenborough documentary.

The glue section was as full as a goog. Super! Instant! Miracle! Fantastic! I told my daughter the marketers for glues were right out of Marvel comics.

She laughed a little.

I held up a tube of superglue. This weapon in the art of the adhesive, superglue, could be slightly dodgy. Toxic as all get-out, it hit like a lightning bolt in the late 1970s with advertisements of cars and even an elephant being lifted via a crane after being bonded by this revolutionary product.

My daughter stared at me.

I explained that superglue was manna to suburban yahoos who didn't really have to worry about skill when it came to repairing stuff.

'Like you?' she asked. Straight-faced. I waggled my finger again and said that of course it rarely worked. But it brought great satisfaction to subeditors who filled up pages of weekend papers with horror stories of people sticking various parts of themselves together and to other objects.

'A bloke I knew swore he stuck himself to a couch when he sat down to watch a football game on the TV and forgot about the tube of superglue in his back pocket,' I said, chuckling.

'Was that you?' my daughter asked.

I stopped chuckling and looked at her. I admitted that, yes, it was me.

'How did you get the couch off you?'

'Well, it was just a cushion. I was going to take the cushion to the hospital, but I rang up instead and they told me to soak myself in nail-polish remover.'

'And that worked?'

I nodded.

'So, you didn't get to hospital with the cushion?'

No, but I did have to take the cushion and myself to the nearest chemist to buy some nail-polish remover.

She started to say something but I simply rolled on and declared, 'So, no superglue!'

I saw an old friend on the shelves, the epically named Tarzan's Grip. An Australian product that had an image of Tarzan the Jungle King prising open a lion's jaws.

It always made me laugh.

I held up the tube to my daughter, pointed to the Jungle King and said, 'Look at that clown, look. What is the fool trying to do with that lion?'

Tarzan's Grip, I told my daughter, was the glue choice of mindless craft classes at school where it was deemed necessary to glue piles of paddle-pop sticks together in odd formations to make wonky-looking boxes or tea mats. You can still see a few entered in the Redcliffe Show.

'All that happened was the glue went everywhere and was so full of chemicals you lost countless brain cells playing with your paddle-pop sticks.' I nodded my head like a sage and continued rambling about glue as my daughter took it all in.

Using it on model aeroplanes was a disaster; the nozzle was too big and you ended up with random bits of Spitfire, Messerschmitt and Mustang stuck to your fingers, ears and face.

Tarzan's Grip's other great attribute was the agonising annoyance when you needed to stick something together and you located a half-tube of Jungle King glue, only to find the cap had been welded tight to the top of the tube with leaking glue. It was impenetrable and therefore useless.

My mother called this occurrence 'Tarzan's gripe'.

I looked up at one product called Gorilla Glue, which boldly proclaimed 'America's Favourite – So Versatile!'

'That is a great name for a glue,' I told my daughter. 'But it's a big call.'

'What does that mean?' she asked.

'Big call to say it's so versatile. Here, anyway, can't speak for America but surely the award for the most versatile sticky stuff must go to the now-vanished Zeus of glues, Perkins paste.'

It was another Australian craft glue that seemed to be everywhere in primary school, in a funny little purple container with little gold medals on it, because, apparently, it was a gold medal–winning glue. The jar wouldn't lie.

'A glue competition? Seriously?' my daughter was slightly skeptical.

'Look it up on your phone, I'll describe it and you tell me if I'm wrong.'

My daughter was up for the challenge.

'Perkins paste had an awkward little white spatula attached to the lid, but it did manage to stick paper cut-outs and pictures onto books and projects.'

She looked at her phone, made a face and said, 'Right, yeah, okay. How do you know this stuff?'

'Because I was there.' I sounded like a conspiracy theorist but I continued.

'And there was always some kid who would eat it. It was made from a potato by-product and I remember a light-eyed boy called Ross eating a few spatulas of it beside me saying he wanted an early lunch.'

'Really?'

'That's versatility for you. Food group and glue.'

'You ate glue?'

'No, I never ate glue, but technically you could, and that kid did. Why, I don't know. No glue should be eaten. He was just, you know . . .' I trailed off.

'What?'

'You know . . .' I nodded my head and she stared back.

'He was a glue-eating fool I went to school with,' I said.

'Is this the same as your friend on the couch? That was you. If it is, just tell me.'

'I have never eaten glue, Ross ate glue,' I said, a little too loudly perhaps. A staff member turned their apron towards us.

My daughter, I felt, was somehow enjoying this, so I continued.

Perkins paste was soon replaced by Clag, another starch-based adhesive. Clag was great because it became a part of your lingo as a kid. If you had a cold, were blocked up and snotty you were, as exemplified by a boy explaining his absence to a teacher, 'All clagged up, crook as, Sir.'

My daughter decided she liked this word Clag. 'Think I'll use that one.'

I thought a bit. About what might have happened to light-eyed Ross and I started laughing. In the glue section.

The staff member who had heard me shouting I was not a glue-eater asked me if I needed help.

I told her I was after an early lunch.

The way she looked at me told me it was time to move on.

My daughter started giggling.

I picked a glue and headed off, and as we left I turned to my daughter and said, 'You know we should come back and see if Bunnings has any creosote.'

'What?' my daughter asked.

'That frame of yours, you know it might need treating. A time for creosote. Another tale I can tell you on another trip to Bunnings.'

'Great,' she deadpanned.

We mended her frame, though in the end, after watching a video my daughter had found on the net, the glue remained unopened in a cupboard. Her method was cleaner and a lot quicker, though I do like to think she picked up a few adhesive gems of wisdom on our trip together.

•

Decisions. Sometimes they are hard to make, and sometimes when you make one it leads you somewhere else and you find, despite yourself, you've taught something to somebody. I made a decision one day and ended up in all sorts of bother for a while and then it seemed to sort itself out and I even manged to teach my children a few things.

Apparently.

I had to decide between two jobs I had been offered and it was giving me a headache. I eventually phoned through my decision to my agent, sat down and stared rather forlornly at an unhelpful laptop screen and wondered if I had made the right decision, which propelled me into another bout of decision-making.

I decided to become cranky.

Cranky, by the way, is a great and underutilised Queensland word. Cranky became increasingly irrational then decisive. I decided to clean my son's room.

I obviously didn't attach much consideration to this resolution.

Lots of teenage boys' rooms are atrocious but I was cranky. I told him if I cleaned it up it'd be a scorched earth policy approach. This was bold talk, for I don't think I understood the size of the matter.

If my son's room were an economic entity it'd be the Greek economy. Epic ruins, chaos, a sense of despair and ancient cultures . . . everywhere.

It was a giant petri dish of exotic moulds and scientifically exciting odours emitting from every nook and cranny.

The United Nations gets a bad rap but the state of that room would have united the General Assembly into decisive action.

Perhaps it was genetic. My parents used to call me Dump Man because I was so messy and I recently bumped into an old housemate who professed that he couldn't quite believe I seemed to have become a civilised and semi-functioning human being.

Pretty rich from a banker.

One day I had just started picking things up, figuring out that it was easier to have some form of order in some part of my life. I was left to come to my own decision and everyone seemed happy about it.

Cleaning up, I decided, wasn't going to prove anything

to my son, sooner or later he'd reach the point when he'd realise that he'd have to start picking stuff up.

But still, I thought, perhaps I should embark on a little mopping-up exercise, make a show of strength and go in for a slight incursion.

I had noticed a distinct lack of towels in the laundry cupboard, and had my suspicions where they might be found. So, nothing too invasive – just mop up a bit, perhaps find some towels. I didn't want to turn into George W. Bush and lose a decade in a quagmire. George never really managed to clean up or pull out of Iraq or Afghanistan, so God knows what his bedroom looked like.

I went in, and all in all I managed to pull out thirty-eight towels.

Talk about a First World problem. Thirty-eight towels. Don't know why anyone, let alone a family of three, would need thirty-eight towels.

Then I discovered a beach towel used by my daughter on a previous Sunday had been tossed in as well. She was in on it too. I'd uncovered a conspiracy, a towel burial site.

Or just someone taking advantage of a convenient opportunity?

This is the point where one decision can lead to another and before you know it you are spouting verse, in a duel with poison-tipped swords, puffy shirts and codpieces. Wait, no, that's *Hamlet*.

In fact, I think I found the body of Polonius wrapped up in a towel somewhere in that room.

But I realised I hadn't really thought this through – if I cleaned his room, what would I have to yell at him about? He is a charming, friendly, gorgeous human being whose only problem is towel management.

So, I decided to leave it at the towels. I banged on about them for a few minutes and left it at that and, after a while, things started to be picked up and put away, some form of order was implemented.

Some years later, my kids, my good friend and I were having a dinner together at a nice restaurant, treating ourselves to a meal and enjoying each other's company.

Nowadays, having inflicted enough damage to my joints and body through succeeding decades of suburban sporting pursuits and fine living, I wear shoes designed to give as much support as possible to the foundations of my large frame – my feet.

My shoes seem to work, are comfortable and get me where I'm going, orthopaedically serene but apparently a fashion nightmare.

Out at dinner and my good friend stared, shook her head and laughed.

'What?' I asked.

'Why do you wear those shoes?'

'They are comfortable,' I said.

My son and daughter laughed.

'Got your special shoes on, Dad? Off to the moon,' said my son.

'Look, they are just shoes,' I proclaimed.

My good friend said I looked like a cross between an old-fashioned deep-sea diver and a fringe festival act. My daughter agreed.

'Nothing fringe festival about me,' I replied, a little too loud.

'No, right in the middle of the road for you, Big Fella!'

It came from another table nearby, an actor who I worked with years ago.

We said our hellos and I asked him what he thought of my shoes. He's more of a wreck than me, so surely would offer some old thespian support.

He looked down at my feet. 'Make sure your air lines don't get blocked down there!'

So, it was laughter on two tables in a nice restaurant. When it was time for me to relieve myself, I stood and did my best deep-sea diver walk to the toilets.

A staff member was soon by my side asking me if I needed assistance, and offering in a confidential tone, 'We have frames here, sir. Walking frames, sir.'

For some reason the tone reminded me of an old British film where a man is walking through a marketplace and a 'local' comes up to him and furtively offers, 'Photographs, sir, lovely photographs.'

Wink, wink, nudge stuff and, although the staff member was sincere, I suppose this is where comfort over fashion taste can take you.

I politely declined and tried to walk normally but I noticed his concerned gaze followed me.

Eyewear is the other hazardous crossing you have to manage on the sea of fashion versus functionality.

I am well and truly at the point in my life when I need a pair of specs on me or near me to function. I have attempted to merge the need to see and the desire for some sort of stylish achievement in taste. I have had a collection of suitably poncy brand names etched into the frames of specs to prove that, at the very least, I had a crack.

Sometimes it works and my good friend will say with a

satisfying level of surprise that what I am wearing on my face looks quite good.

Sometimes it's not worth it. A friend stared at me uneasily after a rugby test we attended had mercifully finished and admitted it wasn't only the score line between the All Blacks and the Wallabies that was disconcerting.

'It's those glasses, Will. And the way you yelled. At best you were like some old documentary about the DLP come to life, but when you screamed at the scrum, it was like Brother Manion trying to teach us Maths in grade nine.'

I had no idea who Brother Manion was, but I wouldn't wish grade nine Maths flashbacks upon anybody, so I apologised, took my brand-name glasses off and promptly tripped over.

When you misplace specs and race into the nearest chemist for a pair of magnifiers, all bets are off. It happened to me when I was working at home on a play once. I was told by my daughter I looked like an image from those pop-up windows you find on the internet. 'Twenty historical images you won't believe.'

This struck me as funny. 'Thank you very much.'

Then my son said something that I think was a compliment. 'It's good, Dad, the way you don't care too much about the way you look.'

And my daughter agreed.

I thought they might be having a go, but no, I was told by my daughter, 'I like how you don't mind how we look, even though you yell sometimes.'

'It's like function over fashion, you give people a little room.'

'Yeah, Big Fella, you cut people a bit of slack to work things out for themselves, like me and my room!' laughed my son.

I sat and thought, they *are* paying me a compliment. My old man's tip for the best way to go about life was to have a crack but cut other people a bit of slack.

I thought that maybe I had done something half right without really knowing how or why.

I wondered to myself if these people, these two little life forms of mine, knew how lovely they'd just made me feel.

I tried to say, 'Well, thank you,' hoping to sound laid-back and unaffected, but it came out as a blubber.

My kids laughed, and they both got up and gave me a cuddle.

•

Sadly, any fantasies of having a father who could gently and calmly impart knowledge in ways of the automobile never landed at our doorstep. My own father was a volatile tutor about matters of the wheel.

He declared to both his sons and daughters that it was easier to teach a charity-box seeing-eye dog new tricks than any of us to drive.

I did attempt to take both my children out on the road. The problem wasn't that I was a bad driver – I am questionable but, touch wood, not a disaster on the roads – but I was a very bad passenger.

I read a pamphlet supplied by a community organisation about calmness being the key to helping your child acquire confidence and knowledge behind the wheel. I attempted this but to little avail, because I winced and jerked and made what I thought were muffled noises. My daughter, though, informed me they sounded like explosions under the water or that I was strangling somebody.

'What do you mean?' I said rather indignantly.

'You. You do this little jerk like you've been electrocuted and then there's all these Jason Bourne grunts as if he's fighting somebody in the dark, trying to keep quiet.'

'Oh, come on.'

Her brother, she said, had warned her about the Vader hand.

'What's that?'

This apparently was when my arm would shoot out and almost touch the windscreen, then ball in and out of a fist, clenching and unclenching. It would suddenly flatten out with my hand extended and point one way and then another as I announced, incoherently, which way we should be travelling, with my underwater-explosion muttered language making no sense.

'You sound like some constipated ventriloquist,' said my daughter. 'It's a little distracting.'

But again, the little life forms learn from watching you.

Misadventures with cars come on many levels. Either they don't start, they break down, cost too much to run or just aren't a right fit. My misadventures tend to happen when I can't find the bloody things. I have forgotten where I have parked my car in carparks, usually airports. Why? I can't give a definite answer. I'm an inattentive ponce who takes things for granted was the theory put forward by a good friend and I can't really argue.

The sad thing is that I have quite often had my son and daughter in tow when this has happened.

They have been witness to me walking aimlessly around in search of my beast, as I utter how surprised I am how many cars look like mine. I suppose the packed volume of cars in a confined place could be a reason why I can't find it, and the fact I just parked and ran in a flap to get the plane.

I mostly locate it with the help of the parking staff and they always seem to channel the patriarch of the old afternoon TV staple *The Brady Bunch* when Mr Brady is about to give a slight admonishment to one of his sons, say Peter. Particularly the episode where Peter doesn't want to play Benedict Arnold in the school play.

Believe me, a 1970s American TV show is so the *vibe*.

With a slow shake of the head (pre-perm Mr Brady, of course, nobody would ever take a permed headshake seriously), the parking attendant reminds me it is important to note down the bay, level and letter number of the parking spot.

One time, the staff member got busy with a little bit of intense Robert De Niro eyeballing and said in a tight whisper, 'Bay. Level. And. Letter.'

I smiled and nodded. He stared. I nodded again and gave a thumbs up. He sighed and we found my car nowhere near where I thought it might be.

Things were more strained in a shopping carpark last Christmas when a clearly harassed manager said to a little group of about four of us who had forgotten where our vehicles were, 'You people. You people. YOU PEOPLE – haven't you heard of Hansel and Gretel?'

My kids and I couldn't help but laugh and got a wagging finger – now that is top-shelf Mister Brady – and a rather admirable comeback sledge.

'They might be fairytales, mate, but at least they knew how to get back to where they needed to be!'

So apart from sprinkling breadcrumbs from my parking bay to wherever I may be headed, I just have to accept that I am a recidivist carpark non-rememberer. A RCNR. I'm thinking of starting up a support group.

There are more of us than you think, I tell my kids, and I like to see other sufferers displaying the telltale signs of the RCNR: the dance of the lost car. The slightly staggered and directionless plod of feet in little circles. The talking to yourself in a repeated mutter, 'Where the hell is it, must be somewhere here.' And then, building to a crescendo of outrage, 'Who designs these bloody carparks!'

The agitated stalk, then the sudden stop and the almost Jedi-like effort to collect your mind power to try and remember where the car is, then the long exhale of breath and the dropped shoulders because you have no clue. All the while a sad little white parking ticket is clutched in your hands.

It was my son who came up with a simple remedy: always take a photo of where you parked the car, bay number, level, general landscape. Perfect, although my own condition reached the point that when I went out of my house to get in my car one morning and couldn't find it, my first thought was, where did I park it?

It took twenty minutes before I realised that it had been stolen.

I turned to my daughter and said happily, 'That's good.'

'What, that the car has been stolen? How is that good?'

'No, it's not good but at least I didn't forget where I parked it.'

Try buying a car. Or selling one. So many ways to purchase and flog a car, so many more platforms to search for a bargain or tempt a buyer. My son recently searched websites and stalked car yards around the suburbs looking for a car to buy.

His first inclination was to follow the family tradition of Volvo ownership. He asked to take an acceptable-looking wagon for a test drive and, after a few hasty muttered words between a mechanic and a salesman, was assured it wouldn't be a problem but that he'd better take an extra battery just in case. He let that one go.

Another wagon appeared on our doorstop a few days later. The owner was an exceedingly pleasant but melancholic man, a bit older than myself, his thin hair in a grey ponytail.

We chatted on the verandah over a coffee. The car, he said, was okay but eccentric.

He told me he was a musician and had been hanging out watching old *Countdown* repeats on *Rage* waiting to see his performance on the show in the 1980s.

I thought this a bit of a stretch, so as we chatted I tapped the name of his band into my phone and let the internet do the work.

'Why don't you watch it on YouTube?' I asked.

'Not the same. I want to watch in situ.'

On my phone, down the time tunnel of the internet came this man with the eccentric Volvo – which sounds like it should be the name of a band.

Instead of the slightly sad, nice man before me was a gyrating, jumping twenty-something with a full head of dark curly hair, *Countdown*-ing it up for all he was worth.

I felt a pang. A lot seemed to have happened to this bloke, but I was reminded by another pity purchase. I once bought a Toyota Crown off an old coot who wheezed and asked me to help him with his medicine, which looked remarkably like small jellybeans.

I felt that pang and even though the car was a lemon – its radio only worked at full bore volume – I said I'd take it.

That old bloke, who'd been like a twitching Lazarus, suddenly jumped up and started clapping me on the back. I had a distinct feeling of being had.

But people can surprise you.

The melancholic musician finished his coffee and advised my son not to buy the car. 'It's not what you're looking for. I've got a daughter, you know, and I was thinking, would I want her driving that car? And I've got to say, no, not really. And anyway, it was nice to get out for a drive.'

'What a top bloke,' my son said as we waved him goodbye. 'Is being a father something that makes you think like that? You know, think about outside yourself?'

I nodded slowly, looking at the eccentric Volvo drive off. 'Yeah, I guess it does.'

I was almost going to cuddle my lovely Clydesdale and then he said with perfect timing, 'Then why aren't you a better bloke, Dad?'

•

Selling's not much easier. My great friend PB recently tried to offload his beloved old Pajero. The Pajero had already been sold once and then returned with a few bits missing as the 'buyer' had changed their mind. PB took back the slightly less complete vehicle and headed for the wholesaler.

Imagining him without his clanking 1992 snorkel-adorned dinosaur is like trying to imagine James Bond without a Vodka martini or Johnathan Thurston playing without his headgear.

PB said his kids were a little worried about how he'd go without his old 'Paj' and he told them that if they'd like to come with him to the wholesaler, it might be nice.

What did he mean by nice?

'Well, a family thing to do. Team effort.'

They were nice kids, so they went.

'There's no goodness in this car,' the wholesaler told PB. 'The goodness was exhausted ten years ago!'

No goodness? PB stood and looked at his kids. No goodness? So, he told the wholesaler about his 'Paj'.

All the experiences he'd enjoyed in that vehicle – driving on the beach at Bribie, on Rainbow Beach and Inskip Point, driving the sands of Moreton Island, through Yellow Patch at low tide, hauling all-wheel drives (a misnomer if there ever was one) out of the talcum powder of Blue Lagoon carpark, traversing Middle Road without missing a beat, teaching his kids to drive 'a difficult vehicle' in the industrial estates of Redcliffe on a Sunday afternoon.

PB was offered a price for all those memories, and his daughter gently put her hand on one of PB's arms and his son gently punched his other arm near the bicep. The wholesaler looked at them. 'I'm a father too, mate, know how you feel.'

PB took a deep breath, made a half-hearted attempt at bargaining and then took the money the wholesaler had offered for old Paj. It wasn't hard; PB had been offered more than the car was worth. Who'd have thought, a car wholesaler with a soft spot for a father supported by his two kids.

A bit later, PB's daughter asked him why exactly he'd said it might be nice for her and her brother to come along to the wholesalers.

'Well, you know. You guys spent a lot of time with the Paj.'

'Dad, it's just a car,' said his son.

'With a sob story attached to bump up the price,' said his daughter.

'And his two kids,' said his son.

PB laughed and said, 'Fathers don't do that . . . much. And you know, team effort.'

He kept the memories but not the hassle. Good to know that sometimes father does know best.

8

MY RIFLE, MY PONY AND ME

*G*etting older puts life in perspective, a friend once told me, then she thought for a bit and said that at least she hoped it did, because there had to be some benefit to growing old.

There's lots of ways to discover that you are getting on in years, not alarmingly, but just a gentle realisation that time's passing.

There's the seemingly random exclamations of noise corresponding to the movement of your body. Rising from a chair or getting out of a car you hear that someone is emitting a sigh, a grunt or an oooooing sound. You look around to see who is making the sound and you realise it's yourself.

Or you might fall asleep in the theatre or cinema or speak quite audibly in the theatre or the cinema. Sometimes you hit the jackpot and combine both in the same outing.

When I sit down in a theatre or cinema I nearly always nod off. And lately I've started to be a bit more audible with exclamations. I went to see a movie with my brother and a couple of his kids, some enjoyable noisy hokum about transforming robots and lots of tiny actors. There was a part with a cheap fright where the camera rolled in slowly on the face of a tiny actor with carefully made up blood and dirt dabbed across his made-up actor's face, with him squinting unblinkingly at some unseen threat, and then suddenly the unseen threat banged down with a crash and roar, just missing the tiny actor.

I got a fright. Lots of people did. I was the only one to scream, 'Christ alive, you bastard!'

My brother looked at me, his mouth open, almost smiling, half sussing me out and half waiting.

I let out a breath and he looked at me again, his mouth slowly closing. His daughter was giggling at me.

A minute later the same tiny actor was walking quietly through some green-screened set, carrying a ridiculously large silver weapon, with a sure sign of heroic endeavour displayed – an arched eyebrow.

There was a sound off screen, the tiny actor swivelled his weapon and his eyebrow went up another few millimetres.

Nothing. He was breathing hard and then . . . Then my brother poked me in my stomach.

'Christ alive, you bastard of a thing!'

His daughter let out a yelp in fright and then doubled up in laughter, as did a few other people in the cinema.

'Oh god, Uncle Bill.'

Up on the screen, the tiny actor's eyebrow went down and he let out a long sigh. 'Nothin' not a goddamned thing,' he said in a tiny-actor tough-guy style.

I looked at my brother. He had his half smile on his face, the sort of look my father had, and then he said, 'Bill, you are just like Dad.'

I looked at him.

'You yell just like Dad in the movies. The spit.'

I looked at my brother, who looked astonishingly like my father, and shrugged my shoulders. 'Gene pool at work,' I replied.

And I attempted to put up some form of rudimentary two-palmed defence to stop any other finger-poking attacks that I was sure were going to come from the seat beside me.

I had never thought of myself as being like my father. I was his son, but I was me, and I always thought there was a fair spread of both my parents in my character. Both were big people who liked to make a bit of noise. That was me. That was my brother and that, I suppose, was my sisters, although they weren't as big as me and my brother.

'Breeding cattle' was my how father had described my brother and me. 'Good Queensland stock, the both of you.'

Most of us go through our days feeling as if we are the central character in the movie. You always think that you are you, unique and simply you.

Or maybe that might be a boofhead thing, something you think until you've lived a bit, when all of a sudden you realise that you aren't just you, but a part of something more.

You. A part of what has come before you.

I remember watching a television show dealing with various celebrities' ancestry and was amused to see the reaction of one subject who desperately wanted some convict's name scratched onto the family tree. Merchants, clerks, the odd clergyman but no convicts.

The look on this person's face was priceless, a desperate disbelieving grimace, the realisation that delving into one's background didn't match up with a self-image.

The parents of a bloke I knew had a Hobbytex tapestry of someone who looked vaguely like a Tudor nobleman because they had traced their family lineage back to the court of the Tudors. They lived in Dandenong in Melbourne, had two large black Citroen DS cars in the drive and a scroll with a hobbyist's calligraphy hand scratching out their noble lines.

I remember asking if the image was of their ancestor and the father said, 'No, that's actually a Henry the Eighth hobby kit. Got the wife to dab it up a bit, but you know it just helps with the family tree feel. It's very authentic.'

So, in one way, family histories can be a search for something that validates and illustrates a person's idea of themselves – a convict, a scandal, a mystery, an Anzac, a bushranger, all dressing up a rather pleasant life in modern Australia.

Can be.

I was invited to speak at a Family and Local History conference where I learnt that a family history can be more than just a Hobbytex kit of pomposity.

The conference was the morning of the christening of my brother's second grandchild and the idea that little Evelyn's name was about to be entered into the records of her life made me think.

I thought of that feeling you get when you see your name on a family tree courtesy of a school project. There, written in my daughter's primary school hand, was me and my date of birth with a line attaching me to her mother, and then two little lines stretching down to her brother and herself.

On her mother's side the family lines went back to the Second Fleet, on my side back to her grandparents. I saw my name marked out as part of a line, this little girl's father. That was me. My role, my part in a story defined.

My daughter asked why there weren't as many names on my side of the family. I remembered my own family tree project from school and how I asked my father the same thing. He was born in Ireland and had met and married a Welsh girl and come to Australia to make their lives, and in a way that was the story he was interested in most. The family he had made with my mother, and the life they had together.

He assured me that whatever names were there they would have been a lot like us. 'They'd have been loud, liked singing and having a gargle.'

I nodded and he went on. 'You, you lot are my story. Your mum and you two boys and three girls, you're all the family tree I need.'

My daughter looked at me when I repeated those words, so I said in my best fatherly manner, 'Quality not quantity, that's the thing.'

She sighed and shook her head.

Family history can be more than just a collection of numbers and names and lines. It's stories of how those names lived, the world they helped make.

A historian friend of mine recently began to study his family and forebears. He was prompted to do this after his father had asked him to go on an historical tour through a graveyard.

My friend told how when he and his father came across the grave of a distant relative, and his father reached for his hand and held it tight, he became reflective and then quite emotional realising he was living a life created in part by what all those names and numbers had created. He left the graveyard quite elated and wanting to find out more about his family.

We all come and go and it's human to try and understand where we fit in. We look to our parents to try and understand a little bit about who we are.

It was odd that my brother had said with such genuine surprise and almost pleasure that I had behaved like my father in the movies. Perhaps he had never seen that before, perhaps as we grow older we distil our behaviour and display a cocktail of our mothers, our fathers. Ourselves.

I know that I had been noticing other character traits that I remember my father displaying. Odd things like clapping his hands when food appeared anywhere he sat to eat it. At picnics, around the dinner table at home, even at a restaurant when we ate out. And he would say, 'A pleasure to meet you,' to what was being served up.

I had found myself occasionally doing this and I would catch myself, realising that I was reminding myself of my father. It was an odd feeling and it seemed to get more pronounced as Christmas grew near.

There is bound to come a time when you think Christmas is a little bit of a drag. You are too busy at work, get swamped by what might be going on and maybe it all becomes a bit tiresome. You've seen what Christmas has to offer and nothing about it is really new. It's a hassle perhaps to deal with the family, buying presents that don't mean that much to anybody; maybe you've just had enough of the rampant commercialism or the spiritual meanings of the season don't strike you as important.

It's easy to feel that way. Too easy, I think.

You don't have to be Ebenezer Scrooge from Charles Dickens' *A Christmas Carol* to look at things with a jaundiced eye.

But what's the point?

Christmas is a chance, if you are willing to take it, to have a little period in the year to say to yourself and others that life is wonderful. There is a sentiment of generosity and a sense of goodwill generated to others in this world that we share.

Life is filled with too many wretched misfortunes, both the random and planned, not to take the time to celebrate the goodness. It's there in the sounds of Christmas, in the memory of home and family. Of friends and strangers.

Howls of laughter at good presents and bad. Of yet another bad bit of clothing, striped t-shirts, socks and jocks, some dreadful piece of nonsense where politeness overtakes honesty and an 'Oh lovely' just hangs in the air from the recipient followed by knowing looks and giggles.

It's clear then that presents don't really matter, what matters is being with the people who matter.

I remember being on a dreadful television show, shooting some awful scene in driving rain. Nobody really enjoyed the job and the weather made it worse.

I asked another actor, who had been the only one not complaining, what kept him content.

'Christmas.'

I just looked at him.

'I do this,' he said, gesticulating at the rain and at the silly make-believe around us. 'And sometimes I feel like throttling people.' He looked at me a little too intently.

'But then I remember Christmas. Warmth, happiness. My kids' faces. I remember it was the one day that my father really loved and let himself enjoy. He used to laugh louder at Christmas. I hear him laughing when he wished people a merry Christmas and, even though he's been dead nearly twenty years, when I wish somebody a merry Christmas or hear other people wish each other Merry Christmas, it's like I hear him laughing. The sound of Christmas makes me happy.'

Nobody said anything and then a grip, a tough grizzled old coot, leant over to the actor, extended his hand and said gently, 'Merry Christmas to you, fella.'

And in the rain, on a miserable set, everyone started wishing each other Merry Christmas and shaking hands. And laughing.

Some say there's no spiritual value to Christmas anymore but there's a lot to find in the tale of the birth of Christ, even if you proclaim no faith. Generosity, redemption, hope.

You look at the world in a kinder way, which allows you to find unexpected gems of delight. I think, remembering my father, you cut people a bit of slack.

At a suburban Christmas carols performance on a staggeringly hot night, the evening's organiser giggled in delight. He had an arm draped around his son's shoulders. His son had also been instrumental in getting the show, a haphazard but spirited affair, together. His son smiled a little. His father whispered something to him.

The old man, I knew, wasn't well, hadn't been for a long while, but he seemed to glow that night, taking in the happy chaos of the concert and looking at his son. He smiled again and bent his head towards his boy.

His son smiled a little. And then I saw the son turn towards his father and give a little hug before mouthing 'I love you, Dad.' Then he moved off to help shift some equipment and tend to a harried-looking St John's Ambulance volunteer with reindeer ears poking out the top of her white cap.

I walked over to the old man and I asked him how he was travelling.

'On a night like this, brother, I am travelling first class.'

I asked him what was amusing him and what he had said to his son.

'Oh, he's a bloody thing he is, getting a bit sooky la la, hey!' he laughed.

Then he breathed in deep, as if he wanted to take in as much of what was going on around him as he could, on this night he had helped organise with his son.

'I love this bloody country. Look, that bloke there,' he pointed to an African Australian man, 'asked that bloke there,' he pointed to a Vietnamese Australian man, 'to move a bit so he can video that bloke up there,' he pointed to a Chinese Australian on stage, 'singing "*white*" Christmas, on a boiling night like this. Bloody magnificent!'

Later in the week, I was flying back from interstate to get back home in time for Christmas. I finished work at six and had a flight at eight. Dumping the hire car at the airport didn't take as long as I thought it might and, by the time I had checked my luggage and made it through security, I worked out I'd have about forty minutes or so in the Qantas Club. Enough time to have a few early drinks to celebrate Christmas, depending how busy it was. I walked in, the crowd was manageable, the bar not too heavily populated. I managed to find a seat in a quieter corner of the club away from the computer, got a drink and a little bowl of wasabi peas.

I put them down on the little table in front of me, I applauded and said, 'Pleasure to meet you.'

I had a sip, picked up a few peas.

'Looks like you needed that.' I looked up and saw a bloke not too far away sitting down, flicking through his phone.

I nodded.

'I actually thought you were talking to me.'

I looked at him and then realised he must have heard me say, 'Pleasure to meet you.'

I held up a hand. 'Sorry, sorry, I was just saying that to the peas, and I, well, look, it's just something my father used to say to, to food, not just peas but to food he was about to eat. Don't know why, but I've found myself doing it occasionally.'

The guy with the phone smiled. 'Fair enough.'

I picked up my glass and raised it to him. 'But you know, it's a pleasure to meet you!'

He smiled again. 'Yeah, Merry Christmas.'

'Same to you,' I said.

We went back to what we were doing, him on his phone, me with newly welcomed peas and a beer, and both of us waiting for our planes. Like everybody else in the lounge, we were waiting to get home for Christmas, and you could hear a few muttered conversations on phones around the lounge.

Messages or muffled discussions about presents remembered, some forgotten, a tone in a voice betraying a surprise that awaited whoever it was at the other end of the phone conversation. Or perhaps they had missed a plane and would be home a little later. They would see the kids tomorrow or maybe they had managed to get an earlier flight and the kids could stay up a little later so they could be surprised.

They were messages I liked.

I had a wasabi pea and thought to myself that transit lounges must have been much quieter places in the days before mobile phones or perhaps people chatted to each other more, or maybe they just waited.

It wasn't just the conversations, it was the ringtones, calling out with snatches of popular songs, or different sounds like dogs barking, old-fashioned ringing, ducks quacking, or Richard Burton speaking.

That one was mine, a snippet of Richard Burton from *Where Eagles Dare*, a hoary old war film from the 1960s where he is trying to radio London from the German fortress he and Clint Eastwood are laying waste to. It's a pretty funny film because our Richard is completely off his chops with dyed hair.

'Broadsword calling Danny Boy, over,' he intones in a voice straight from the Royal Shakespeare Company and years of boozing, cigarettes and good living.

If he kept repeating his phrase it was a call, but if I only got one 'Danny Boy' then it was an email, text or voice message.

The man who had wished me a merry Christmas laughed and shook his head.

'You are joking, a *Where Eagles Dare* ringtone. Brilliant.'

I nodded, always happy to recognise a fellow traveller in the ways of bad popular culture. He knew the worth of 'Broadsword calling Danny Boy'.

'My father loved that film, in fact that was the first film he bought as a VHS cassette,' he said.

'A top-shelf purchase,' I said.

'Actually, it's probably due for another viewing.'

'Christmas is the right time for a bit of Burton and Eastwood mayhem,' I said.

The man laughed a little. I picked up my phone, two messages. One from my daughter saying she was going over to a friend's place for the night and could I pick her up tomorrow on the way to the beach. 'Love you heaps,' she had typed at the end of her message.

I smiled and texted back. 'Ditto, see you 10ish.'

Then for the message from my son. I took a sip of my drink. He was on a trip to the US with some of his mates, driving across the country, so messages from him recently were few and far between.

'Driving through Amarillo listening to "My Rifle, My Pony and Me". Very cool. Love you.'

I read it again.

Just a couple of sentences, if that, but sometimes a few words can mean a lot. I looked at the message again and I let out a sigh.

I reached for my drink and my new *Where Eagles Dare* chum was peering up from his phone.

I looked at him.

'All good?' he said and he grimaced a bit. 'Sorry,' he went on, 'just that sigh was a bit big. Don't mean to pry.'

He didn't seem like a bad sort of a bloke.

'No, all good.' I thought I'd tell him, he was probably a father himself.

'Sigh was a bit about pre-Christmas logistics tomorrow. Pick up my daughter from a mate's place, pick up the Christmas ham from Eddie's the butcher then get down the beach and get the tree and make sure we've got the pressies we need.'

'That's a day,' said my new chum.

I nodded and looked at my phone again. 'The second message was from my son. He's on a road trip with a couple of mates, so he's having too much fun to contact me much but,' I stopped and I held up my phone, 'but that was a good message to get.'

The man put down his own phone and asked, 'Why?'

I thought about getting another drink but instead I thought about what I'd tell my new chum from the lounge.

I could have told him about how I'd been working away in Brisbane for a bit and how my daughter had finished her VCE year with me away but had done well. And how, even despite that, my absence had made me feel a bit guilty. I hadn't been around when she had received her final VCE score, which had seemed such a big deal, all that pressure heaped on kids in their final year of high school.

That number seems so important, a make or break moment. And when I called, she had seemed down. I had told her that no matter what score she received I loved her and was very proud of her. Then she took a deep breath and told me with a trembling voice her score.

And then she'd laughed. And her aunt, my sister-in-law, whose place she was staying at, had laughed along with her.

It was a high score and she had well and truly had me going. She laughed and told me it was very sweet what I had said to her about being proud and loving her. 'You're a dag,' she said.

This was the girl who had liked to play a prank or two. When she was a toddler and we were down the beach I had been reading the paper and she was paddling about. When I looked up and noticed she was gone, I called her name. No reply. I got up and asked some friends who were staying with us if they had seen her. They said they hadn't. When I couldn't find her, I'd felt an awful gripping fear. I yelled out her name and ran around the house and yard calling her name. No reply.

I ran into bedrooms I had already checked and called for her, I fell to the floor and looked under a bed. And there she was, smiling at me. I could have throttled her, but I picked her up, this giggling child, and cuddled her so hard I thought she might pop, but she just giggled.

I could have told him that but I didn't.

I could have told him that my son being overseas had given me kittens. Made me sick with worry. When I said goodbye to him at the airport I had tried not to but then couldn't help myself and had cried.

He had laughed his big laugh and told me he'd be fine and my daughter had shaken her head but held my hand.

I didn't tell him that either.

But that message. I could tell him about that message and how much it meant to me.

This song, 'My Rifle, My Pony and Me', was from an old Western movie called *Rio Bravo* with John Wayne, Dean Martin and Ricky Nelson.

It was one of those films that seemed to have a permanent place on the roster on television on a Sunday afternoon, one of those movies that even your father would watch.

Big Duke and drunken Dean and the young gunslinger Ricky Nelson go up against a town of bad guys and somehow pull it off. I liked it in part because my father seemed to be so into it, for usually he'd be off banging nails into some wall around the house, or daubing timber with creosote or burning stuff in his incinerator.

But he'd pull up a pew and sit down and watch. 'This flick is all right, worth a watch.'

There was a scene when the trio and some old coot with a harmonica are hanging around the sheriff's office before they swagger off down the dusty main street to face the bad guys, and Dean Martin and Ricky Nelson sing a soft, lilting cowboy song.

'My Rifle, My Pony and Me'.

They sing it without accompaniment, a pretty evocative song with Dean Martin's warm baritone softly crooning in tandem with Ricky Nelson's lighter voice.

It was a tune that my father would hum or whistle occasionally. Near the end of a day, perhaps walking down to the beach for a swim, or out the back as the sun was setting and the sky was burning a golden orange before slowly darkening.

The song is about a cowboy resting for a night in a canyon dappled in evening's purple light and as the cattle he is droving settle down by a stream he stops his work for the day and beds down for the night. After his day's work, he thinks about the people he loves.

It's a wonky old movie, but it was one of those films about men standing up and doing what good men should do, from a less complex and more naïve time. The sort of time when men like my father thought of cowboys as knights of the plains doing honourable deeds as they went about a frontier life.

There was a lyric in that song my father would sometimes say to me as he would pass my room as I was going to bed, his big frame leaning in the doorway, 'Come on, it's time for a cowboy to dream.' And he would say goodnight.

I had played the song once to my son and told him about how my father had whistled it when he was winding down from the day and how it made me think of my dad whenever I heard it played.

There was a line in the song about heading to Amarillo.

The man in the lounge looked at me.

'And your boy played the song with his mates as they're driving through the States?' he said.

I nodded. 'It's like my old man is sort of with him, which I know is sort of silly but you know,' and I trailed off.

'Or how you're with him as he's heading through Amarillo,' said the man in the lounge. 'He's thinking about you. Mate, that's pretty cool.'

I hadn't thought about it that way and I looked at the message again. Maybe that's why he sent it.

I looked at the man and nodded my head a little, and then I thought it polite to enquire about him. 'You got kids?'

He smiled a little and then shook his head.

No, he said, he and his wife didn't have any children. He was quiet for a bit and seemed to be thinking if he should go on. I supposed he must have thought I was as good as anybody else to have a chat with; after all, I had just bent his ear more than I'd ever imagined I would. He took a deep breath and he said, 'Didn't work out for us. Which was a bit tough but, you know, that's the way things panned out.'

There was a pause and he went on.

They had tried to have kids, they both expected to, but it had been difficult. They had, he said, 'Gone off and tried just about everything there was to try, but it just didn't happen. It just didn't happen.

'It's what it is, you know, we'll go off at Christmas, spoil our nieces and nephews and friends' kids rotten, make a fuss and it will be fun. It's okay. Sometimes a little tough – but it's okay.'

After a little bit, I told him I was sorry.

He shrugged his shoulders slightly and nodded. 'Thanks. There's always *Where Eagles Dare* to watch with my dad. In Blu-ray.'

I laughed.

Then he sighed. 'I said to my wife I was sorry, but she told me nobody was to blame. Just the way things worked out.'

I nodded.

Then a flight number heading to Melbourne was called out.

I began to get my stuff together. 'Well, mate, that's me,' I said.

He nodded. 'I'm on the delayed to Adelaide,' and he went on, a little embarrassed, 'Listen, I'm sorry, I don't blurt like that. It's just your kids and, you know. They seem good.'

'They're all right, could throttle them sometimes but you know, I love 'em.'

'Yeah,' and he nodded. 'Yeah, that's good.'

'Merry Christmas,' I said to him.

'Merry Christmas,' he replied.

I was on my way out of the Qantas Lounge when I heard him say, 'Hey.' I stopped and turned; he'd followed me.

'Look, I wonder if you could do me a favour. I'm sorry, but would you mind just wishing them a merry Christmas from me? My name is Rob.' He winced. 'Is that stupid?'

I said no it wasn't and we shook hands.

I walked away.

Out of the lounge and down towards my departure gate.

I realised I hadn't even finished my drink or the wasabi peas that I'd said it was a pleasure to meet.

Maybe it was a bit stupid for a bloke I'd never see again to wish my kids a merry Christmas. We'd just chatted for a while, that's all, chatted as we waited for our planes.

I stood in line and shuffled forward down the air bridge and into the plane and I remembered another Christmas.

I remembered that once, when my children were quite small, I returned from working interstate on Christmas Eve.

I walked through the gate and up the stairs. On the first step, when my boot landed on the wood, I heard little voices cry from the back of the house and the dog barking.

I stood at the front door, heard footsteps of little people running up the hallway. The skittering paws of our hound. And when I opened the door little arms grabbed me, clung to me. I staggered to a halt. Our dog barked, leapt and licked.

My kids buried their faces into either side of my body. I felt their little bodies fluttering as they clung to me, like the way beautiful delicate creatures might, like butterflies held in your hand. I looked up and saw my wife smiling from the end of the hallway.

There was the smell of the Christmas tree and the feeling of being home with people I loved. It was a communion of what mattered most to me in my life.

How could I ever forget such a Christmas moment? That's what life can be like when you're a father.

I sat in my chair. No, it wasn't stupid what he had asked me to do in the lounge.

Before I was told to put my phone into flight mode, I texted my son and my daughter. I passed on the message. Merry Christmas from Rob.

And I'd tell them what it meant when I saw them.

I fastened my seat belt and, after a while, as we lifted into the sky, I hummed a sweet evocative little tune to myself because it was time for a cowboy to dream. My rifle, my pony and me.

aCKNOWLEDGEMENTS

I would like to acknowledge, in no particular order of importance, the following people: Robert 'Bowtie' Watkins, Karen Ward, Deonie Fiford, Anna Egelstaff, all at Hachette, Bernadette Foley, Bevan Bleakley, Rick McCosker, Paleface Adios, Peter Bolton, Clem McInnes, Stella McInnes, Amanda Higgs, Ray and Delilah.

hachette
AUSTRALIA

If you would like to find out more about Hachette Australia, our authors, upcoming events and new releases you can visit our website, Facebook or follow us on Twitter:

hachette.com.au
facebook.com/HachetteAustralia
twitter.com/HachetteAus